KISSES ON A POSTCARD
A Tale of Wartime Childhood

Terence Frisby

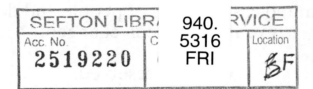
WINDSOR
PARAGON

First published 2009
by Bloomsbury Publishing
This Large Print edition published 2010
by BBC Audiobooks Ltd
by arrangement with
Bloomsbury Publishing Plc

Hardcover ISBN: 978 1 408 45954 6
Softcover   ISBN: 978 1 408 45955 3

British Library Cataloguing in Publication Data available

Printed and bound in Great Britain by CPI Antony
Rowe, Chippenham and Eastbourne

To Jack and Rose Phillips, our foster parents during the Second World War, who gave my brother and me three rich years of childhood while the world destroyed itself around us. We will be grateful to them till our dying breaths, which now can't be that far away.

FOREWORD

What memoir of childhood could be entirely true, written through the wrong end of the telescope? There are always reconstructions, guesses, elaborations, omissions. On top of any unintentional inaccuracies I have to own up to inventing certain characters and changing a few names and events to protect people—and, possibly, their descendants—who were once very kind to two small boys. And even to protect those who weren't.

But some of the deliberate changes of the story and characters are there for a different reason, which is all to do with the way this book came into existence.

It started as twenty-two pages of reminiscences. The BBC commissioned me to turn those pages into a ninety-minute play for Radio 4. I am a playwright, and play-writing is about architecture. Without a shape, you don't have a play, so I shaped my reminiscences into a narrative that would hold together through a beginning and middle to a proper climax. Also, to make a play (well, certainly a radio play) you need dialogue. Nobody could possibly remember, verbatim, conversation after conversation that took place many years ago and which I reproduced for the radio. They are from my imagination, based on my memories of what actually took place. This play, entitled *Just Remember Two Things: It's Not Fair and Don't Be Late*, won the Giles Cooper award, The Best Radio Play of the Year, 1988.

The success of the radio play led to the next

step, which was a stage musical at the Queen's Theatre, Barnstaple. It had twenty-three children and twenty-two adult actors in the cast. Once again I further doctored the literal truth to fit a musical play. After all, how many people suddenly burst into song in real life—though I certainly did. But I assert fiercely that I have remained true to the people and memories of my wartime childhood.

When I finally decided to write the story as a book, I had to decide: do I cut out my inventions and go back to the bare facts or stay with the narrative I had shaped them into? There was only one answer. Anyway, after writing the two scripts, my version of the story is as real to me now as what might have actually happened nearly seventy years ago. So perhaps I should call this a re-creation of my childhood. However, I can say, hand on heart, that nearly every one of the people in this book existed as I have drawn them, most of the events happened and all of my story is truthful to their memory and the spirit of their lives.

This is a thank-you letter, if you like, to the people of Doublebois and Dobwalls and—especially—to Jack and Rose Phillips, Auntie Rose and Uncle Jack to us and the whole of Doublebois, an extraordinary, ordinary couple who seem to me to embody everything good in working-class people of that time. Although none of us ever mouthed such sentiments then, we loved them and were loved by them.

Let me not omit our mother and father, whose concern for their two sons gave birth to the original, imaginative *Kisses on a Postcard* idea. Every last word of that part of the story is utterly true.

CHAPTER ONE

I was the luckiest of children: I had two childhoods.

My earliest memories are of pre-war antiseptic Welling, just in Kent but really suburban London. The world I first lived in was even younger than I was, street upon street of it, all built since my birth in 1932. This brave new one-class creation consisted of red-brick, pebble-dashed houses— semis or four-in-a-row—bought on mortgages by young couples who had managed to raise the £25 deposit. With their small children they had escaped from the grime of Deptford, Woolwich Docks and New Cross (where I was born) through the newly legislated green belt, to fresh air and gardens. Our garden, according to my father, was the biggest in Eastcote Road. Because of a slight bend in the road a spare wedge had been tacked on to our plot. My father was perpetually proud of the imagined status his extra square yards bestowed on him and we assimilated our share of his pleasure.

In spite of the gardens, we kids lived in the street. Children were everywhere, gangs of us on every second corner. Those new-laid, spacious-to-us, concrete streets were our playground. A ball and a bike were essentials from an early age. A motor vehicle was a rarity when it disturbed our games of football, cricket, or 'aye-jimmy-knacker', a pitiless physical team game that involved one team bending over in a line at right angles to a wall, locked together, head between the legs of the boy in front, while the other team, one by one, vaulted heavily on to their backs to make them collapse. When the whole team was mounted the riders of this tottering heap chanted, 'Aye-jimmy-knacker, one, two, three, aye-jimmy-knacker, one, two, three, aye-jimmy-knacker, one, two, three. All men off their horses.' If any of the riders fell off, their team lost. If the boys underneath collapsed, they lost and had to bend over again. If they didn't, they had won that round and had their turn as riders. And so on and bruisingly on. The smallest boy in each team stood with his back to the wall with the head of the first boy cushioned in his stomach, at first sight the cushiest place to be until the thumping riders landed and the head was driven into you with, literally, sickening force. I remember the feeling well: I was frequently the smallest boy.

No cars were parked in those streets because none of our parents owned one. In Eastcote Road of nearly a hundred houses there were perhaps three, primly stowed in their garages, or standing gleaming on the garden path of the smug owner. We were interrupted more often by the milkman's or greengrocer's or coal-merchant's horse and cart, and by the occasional steaming pile of manure left behind, snapped up for his dad's flower beds by the first one there with a bucket and shovel.

We rode our bikes wildly round our empty streets in a wheeled version of hide-and-seek, which we called tracking, then more sedately out on to the main roads, with expeditions to Danson Park, up Shooters Hill (and tearing madly down again, nearly out of control), into the extensive

4

woods: Oxleas, Jack and Crown. 'No Bicycles' it said on the notices, but that was of no interest to us. We rode further afield to Blackfen, Woolwich Ferry, Blackheath, Eltham swimming baths and down the A2 bypass to haunted Hall Place, near Bexley.

I was six when I got my first proper bike to join in this fun. It was a fat-tyred affair blackmailed out of my parents, who foolishly promised me a two-wheeler when I could ride one. Since infancy I had ridden a tricycle, a trike, which I had grown to despise. Presumably they thought they had me in a catch-22 situation: no bike, can't learn; can't learn, no bike. But I borrowed one and took it to the top of Ashmore Grove, where two friends balanced me on it and shoved me off. I stayed on long enough down the hill to crash the bike into the gutter and run home to announce to my parents that I could ride. As soon as I had my own bike I made my brother Jack's life a misery by following him and his friends everywhere. He was four years four months older and regarded me as an embarrassing, unwanted accessory. They could have left me behind eventually, but I could stay with them long enough to get out of our estate and ensure that Jack wouldn't leave me pedalling furiously on my fat tyres, alone and at the mercies of main-road traffic. So I was waited for and reluctantly included, happy beyond words to be on my bright-red new (second-hand but new to me) bike, out with the big boys.

*   *   *

Dad, lower-middle-class Dad, worked on the

5

railway, a carriage-trimmer, later an undermanager, then, post-war, boss of the carriage-and-wagon repair depot at Stewart's Lane, Battersea. He had been a successful amateur boxer, a local welterweight champion and contender for national ABA titles. He encouraged us both to box, just to look after ourselves. All of us boys in those streets were in and out of fights constantly. When Jack came home one day in tears because a bigger boy had hit him, Dad offered him sixpence to go and hit the boy back, no matter what happened subsequently. I can't remember what Jack did but I went and hit the boy's younger brother, about my size, came home, demanded and got my sixpence. But boxing didn't take with either of us. Dad was a member of the Labour Party, a trade unionist, a physically strong, aggressive, hard-working man who could frighten us by the force of his personality and his occasional tempers. He was also very sentimental, gentle, loved to make us laugh and—as did our mother— made us feel secure and special. This was expressed one day when he came home from work carrying a piece of varnished wood with the word 'JackTer' cut into it and painted gold. This he screwed into the lintel over the front door and everytime Jack and I went in and out we were reminded that our house was named after us.

Mum came from a family which had all the appearance, speech and style of the upper middle class—without the income. They were mostly professional musicians, all of them female by the time I was around. The males had died or disappeared and one great-uncle was in jail in Canada for some white-collar crime. Mum played

6

the piano and would bash out jazz and popular tunes with a strong rhythmic left hand—stride, it was called, because of the way the left hand strode up and down the keys controlling everything. I loved it when she played: the little rituals of lifting the lid of the piano stool to get the music out, the deliberateness with which she took her seat—no concert pianist did it better—the fiddling removal of her rings, placed carefully at the upper end of the keyboard, and then the house was filled with rhythm and joyous noise. Both of our parents came from Brighton. She had been a professional jazz drummer there in the 1920s. Yes, that is what she was, possibly the only female jazz drummer in this country, unique. She played all over Sussex at country-house dances and at various venues in Brighton. At a dance at the Ship Hotel one Saturday night my father stared long and hard at the drummer and, knowing her, she almost certainly glanced back and wielded her drumsticks with extra panache. When the band broke for the interval and records were played he was the only one with enough nerve to ask the MC if he could have a dance with the drummer.

They got married and her new husband's job on the Southern Railway took them from the Brighton depot to New Cross in South London. She told me years later that she couldn't believe what she had done to her life: from being a local celebrity, playing at dances in the town and glamorous balls in Sussex country houses, she had become a wife living in a Victorian flat on his modest wages with two small sons in one of the poorer bits of South London. When we moved on to Welling it must have been a bit of an

7

improvement, but the cultural desert of north-west Kent was no replacement for fun-filled, shameless, gaudy Brighton-on-Sea, home of the dirty weekend and chosen residence of so many glamorous figures since the Prince Regent built his pleasure dome: the glorious, dotty Indian Pavilion with its Dome, where she and various members of her family had frequently played.

Visits to Brighton to see both our parents' families were always exciting. First, there was the journey, a thrill enough on its own: a suburban electric train to Charing Cross, with the wonderful stretch between New Cross and London Bridge where eight or ten lines ran parallel and your train seemed to race others into the station; the occasional steam engine might also roar or chug past; out of Charing Cross station into the Strand; onto a bus through Trafalgar Square, where you could twist your neck to see Nelson on top of his column; down Whitehall and soberly past the Cenotaph with its sombre meaning, much fresher then than now; motionless guards like your toy soldiers outside St James's Palace; another opportunity to get a crick in your neck as we passed Big Ben and Parliament; along Victoria Street to another station, Victoria, part of our railway world; then the main event, a fifty-two-minute, non-stop ride on the Brighton Belle, our train: it took us back over the Thames for the second time, past the engine sheds at Battersea and Nine Elms, speeding through south London, into Merstham Tunnel and out into the ersatz Surrey countryside, really glorified suburbs, which developed into the Sussex Weald, proper farmland. The invariable exclamation from our parents, 'Look. It's the South Downs.' This was the climax, the dramatic skyline of the Downs, the bare grassy slopes like a sleeping Gargantua rising out of the soft fields, always pointed out to us though we knew it by heart. I think Mum, in particular, felt she was arriving home when she saw the South Downs. The train dived under them in a tunnel and suddenly you were out into Brighton and the brassy seaside.

Dad's mother lived in Stanley Road up the hill behind the fire station in an ordinary Victorian terraced house. It was only several minutes' walk from the station, at the back of the town. His father, former chef at the Grand Hotel, was dead. Drink was involved somewhere. As a result, Dad, though not entirely teetotal, was a very light drinker all his life. On the other hand, Mum loved the whole social business of going out for a drink and 'enjoying yourself'. This difference in their tastes did not help an already difficult relationship. At the top of our grandmother's road was a children's playground to which Jack and I ran as soon as we could. Aged four, I broke my arm there on a roundabout and was being carried back to Granny's while somebody sped down the road to the fire station, where my father was chatting to a friend. I remember clearly, and it became family legend, that the messenger rounded the corner at the bottom of the road running flat out as Dad, also running flat out (back towards me), appeared in the same instant as if he were making a well-rehearsed relay takeover. He took me in his arms and sprinted back down to the fire station. It was a jolting, painful ride, I remember, though I am sure he held me carefully. The firemen tied my arm

9

between two rulers as splints and put it in a sling. An ambulance arrived, bell clanging, to take me on another ride, this one exciting in spite of the pain, to hospital, where I was anaesthetised while my arm was set. I had it in plaster for a while, proudly, until it started to itch like mad.

It was the visits to Mum's relatives that were the grand, sophisticated occasions. Indeed, it was one of them, her Auntie Molly, who had found the £25 deposit to put down for our house. My great-aunt Molly was the pretty one of the three aunts who brought Mum and her sister up—their mother had been packed off to Canada after some sort of scandal and had a second family there. All three great-aunts (and my absent, possibly disgraced grandmother) had been suffragettes and were very much free feminist thinkers before the turn of the century. They were well educated, cultured and all spoke with beautifully clear Edwardian diction. 'Off' was 'orf' in their language and if they called themselves or someone else 'a silly ass' it rhymed with pass with no anatomical overtones. I remember one of them saying to me in answer to my enthusiastic endorsement of a children's film, 'Grown-up life's not like that. Films and plays are too tidy. Life's much more messy. We're all silly asses in the end.' The word that I thought I had heard from such lips shocked me so much that the remark's content has stayed with me along with the pronunciation.

Molly was a classical double bassist. After one local scandal and more than one *affaire* she married a prosperous furrier so was able to keep her two penniless sisters. The younger one was sweet, vague Auntie Clare, who played the violin

10

and viola and had a lifelong *affaire* with an equally broke violinist. When he died he left her all his possessions, a cupboardful of violins, not one of them a Stradivarius. I enjoy using the period word '*affaire*' for their love lives because that is the *mot juste*; it was listening to their gossip that I first heard it, voice lowered, second syllable slightly stressed, and wondered what it meant. The older penniless sister was crabby Aunt Millicent, a virgin I am sure, who had taught algebra and Greek at Cheltenham Ladies' College and intimidated Mum and her sister throughout their childhood. They all lived in a grand, spacious Edwardian house, 47 The Drive, the best address in Hove, with the sea at the end of the road. Again we could feel special. Molly and husband—who used to hand Jack and me munificent half-crowns when we visited—occupied the main, sumptuous body of the house, Clare and Milly in the basement flat. The general conclusion among Mum's all-female relatives was that she had married beneath her. Nevertheless, they showed sympathy rather than censure.

A cherished memory of Mum (of so many) is of her standing in the kitchen in Welling with Jack and me sitting at the table, the radio on, Borodin, Rimsky-Korsakov or Stravinsky or Ravel or Debussy or Tchaikovsky playing; she holding a cooking implement, waving her arms and hands about, a faraway smile on her face. She would undulate in her version of a harem-type dance, saying, 'Listen, boys, listen. It's beautiful, isn't it? See? The Russians and the Romantics and the Moderns. Aren't they lovely? Just listen.' And I have, ever since.

The day before the Second World War started (it was a Saturday) Dad shovelled Mum, Jack and me off to safety in Portslade, near Brighton, to stay with Mum's sister and family in another 1930s house similar to our own. Great-aunt Molly probably paid the deposit on that one too, treating the sisters equally. Safety? We would have been right in the path of any invading Germans. Auntie Esme (a former cellist who had sailed to South Africa and back, scraping away) was married to Uncle Walter; they were a very happy pair; their children were our cousins, David, Audrey and Maureen.

I listened to the famous declaration-of-war broadcast by Neville Chamberlain at 11 a.m. on that first Sunday in September 1939 with Mum, Auntie Esme and Maureen. Something like panic reigned. Dad, Uncle Walter, Jack, David and tomboy Audrey had gone out for a walk on the foreshore (you could scarcely call the undistinguished bit of coastline at Portslade a beach). Would they be back before the Germans landed? Was our fear for them or for ourselves, left undefended at home? Maureen and I scuttered anxiously up and down the street looking for them, told to venture no further by Mum and Auntie Esme, who were peering out of the front door as all the church bells in the land tolled out their dreadful warnings. I saw the four of them some way off, strolling towards me in animated conversation, and ran anxiously up to them yelling, 'Did you see any Germans?' I was greeted with bafflement, then derision.

During the autumn of the Phoney War we cousins privately started the real thing between ourselves. We brawled incessantly. Auntie Esme and Mum, who were very close and loved their reunion, tried to ignore us, while Uncle Walter, tall, gangling, gentle Uncle Walter, decided to bring us all together with a cooperative project. Under his leadership we all embarked on the doomed attempt to build an air-raid shelter in the back garden. This trench, dug with so much effort into the solid clay that was under the garden, was always half full of water and was a glorious place to fight with our cousins and produce quantities of mud that horrified even our hardened mothers. Uncle Walter lived above the squalls and skirmishing in a quiet world of his own from which he tried, with no success, occasionally to remonstrate with an errant child. Dad was absent from Monday to Friday: 'essential war work' on the railway in London was the hushed, reverent explanation.

I remember one dispute that left me with a sense of the injustice of life. We were at table for a meal. Maureen, our youngest cousin, picked up a spoon and whacked me over the head with it. I could find nothing else to hand except a knife, so I picked it up and whacked her back, being careful even at my tender years to hit her with the flat and not the blade. It made no difference; Maureen yelled and retribution clattered about my ears as Mum and Auntie Esme joined forces to bombard me with outrage for using a knife on my little cousin. She got away with her attack scot-free— and cut-free too because of my unappreciated care.

One result of us children being herded together at bedtime was that I got my introduction to sex. Jack and I, having no sister, must have seemed pretty naive to our mixed cousins. One night we played the 'I'll show you mine if you'll show me yours' game. I cannot remember who suggested it but it certainly wasn't me and I do not believe Jack would have dared to do such a thing. Anyway, we shyly pulled down our pyjama trousers and solemnly gazed at each other. Maureen, aged five, said, 'Look,' reversed herself, bent over, head upside down between her knees, eyes looking up at us through her legs, and gave us a grandstand view of her back bottom. Jack and I stared, fascinated as much by the gesture as by the sight before us. 'Oh Maureen,' said Audrey wearily, as though this happened frequently, but I felt a rebuke was out of place; Maureen's action was daring, generous and stylish; she offered more than she was getting. Perhaps she was just being exhibitionist but I don't think so. She became my favourite cousin.

We were—as was promised to the soldiers of the previous world war—home by Christmas. It was a relief to all of us, each family being mightily relieved to be rid of the other, though Mum and Auntie Esme were sorry to be parted again.

Back in Welling the Phoney War continued, a few months of a sort of pre-war existence, except that now there were shortages of everything that had been available even in a Britain barely emerging from the Great Depression. In anticipation of air raids barrage balloons hung above us over Shooters Hill golf course, great useless bags of gas that were supposed to deter low-level attacks and did absolutely nothing as far

14

as anyone can remember. Occasionally one broke free and sailed away on the wind, trailing its cables, which hit the odd pylon or overhead electrical wire and created havoc and power cuts. The balloons always came down in the most inconvenient places, giving photo-opportunities to enterprising local reporters and the chance of a great deal of comedy business to the soldiers who were sent to retrieve them. Where possible the troops attached them to lorries and towed them back, followed by packs of cheering, jeering boys on bicycles.

Up in Oxleas Wood, a few hundred yards from our house, anti-aircraft guns, searchlights and rockets were hidden in the trees. The long menacing shapes of the barrels of the ack-ack guns poked up through the leaves and branches. The beams of the searchlights waved about hitting the underside of clouds or continuing to infinity as the Observer Corps trained on them at night. But when the rockets were fired the shattering whooshes and roars seemed to open the doors of hell. We cowered in our beds, aghast, our stomachs turning to water, even though we knew they were on our side, and pitied any Germans who would dare to come near. To have close looks at these alien, thrilling objects we children invaded those parts of the woods that were fenced off and marked 'Private' only to be good-naturedly driven off by the soldiers and chased with less amiability by the park keepers.

One of them caught us one day and gave us a severe lecture. 'Before you kids came here nightingales sang in these woods. Where are they now, eh?' I went home and reported this to Mum.

15

Her mouth set in a hard line. Never one to take on authority directly, she put on her coat, went and found the keeper and harangued him on the subject of how much disturbance he thought regiments of soldiers created as they erected campsites and tested their guns in comparison to a few kids trying to creep about and not be caught. I don't know what the keeper said in answer, if anything, but he still went on chasing us. It wasn't long before those guns and rockets were in nightly use. No nightingales have since sung in Oxleas Wood to my knowledge.

Then in May 1940, the Second World War broke out in earnest as far as Britain was concerned: the Germans attacked; their panzer divisions swept through the Low Countries and France; the British and French armies were brushed aside; the disaster-cum-deliverance of Dunkirk happened, and what I call my 'other childhood' began. Jack, aged eleven, and I, aged seven, became evacuees—vackies—and were carried off to another world.

CHAPTER TWO

We were all up early that morning, 13 June 1940. Two little brown cases were already packed, sandwiches and pop at the top for easy access. Dad was first to leave, off to work. I don't remember him hugging or kissing us; men didn't go in for that in those days. He may have shaken our hands. What he did do, to demonstrate his authority and reassure us, was to tell us that he knew where we were going, but he could not tell us because it was

16

a war secret—a heavy wink accompanied this—and we would like it there. It would be in the country, fun; perhaps even—dare we hope it?—the seaside. No, he wasn't going to tell: wait and see. We were to be sure to look out on the left just after Wandsworth Road station as our train would go over his office, which was in the arches under the railway there, and he would wave. We knew then that we would be on a train that would leave Welling and cross south London, on to the Western Section, not a scheduled route of our Eastern Section suburban services to Waterloo, Charing Cross and Cannon Street. We knew our train would be special. We were railway children and proud of it and of our privileged knowledge. And if Dad knew we were taking that route he must be privy to the whole secret evacuation plan.

'It'll be a steam engine.' Another clue that we were going well out of our electrified world, an impressively long journey. We knew the exact stations where electrification terminated in all directions.

'Cor, what? A namer? What?' we asked, excited. 'Schools-class?'

'Don't think it'll be a schools class,' he said. 'Not big enough for your journey: only a 4-4-0.' He dismissed an engine which pulled the Dover boat trains and we loved, a compact modern design sitting on its four driving wheels and four bogies. We often saw them on trips up to Charing Cross on our Eastern Section of the railway, cosier than the bigger Western Section locomotives used for the longest routes out of Waterloo. 'Could be a King Arthur.' This was a 4-6-0 express with three drivers a side. 'Maybe even a Lord Nelson.'

17

Another 4-6-0, the biggest engine on the Southern Railway, only used for the West of England runs. We digested this with a sense of importance as he went off to work.

Mum had a tie-on label in her hand with my name and address on it in block capitals. 'Here, let me put this on you,' she said.

'Ah, no. I know who I am.'

'That's in case the Germans capture you,' said my knowing brother.

'Honest?' I was fascinated.

'Don't be silly, Jack. Come here.' Mum was sharp. She had another label for him.

'I haven't got to wear one too, have I?' Jack was disgusted.

'Yes, both of you.'

The two labels also had our school, class and teacher on the reverse side. I was being evacuated with Jack's school, Westwood, a large secondary school over a mile away, although I was still at Eastcote Road Primary, right opposite our house. Whoever had devised the evacuation scheme had the good sense to try to keep younger brothers and sisters with their older siblings.

While we objected, she tied them through the buttonholes in the lapels of our jackets. As I look now at all those old photos and films of vackies boarding trains and buses in their thousands in 1940, it leaves a hole in my stomach to consider how our mothers felt, tying labels on the most precious things in their lives and sending them off like parcels to God knows where, with the threat of annihilation from the air or sea hanging over us all. But our mother showed no sign of worry. She had two serious points to remind us of. The previous night at bedtime she had drilled them into us.

'Terry, you've got to do as Jack says. Do you hear me?'

'Oh no.'

'Oh yes. And you stay with him all the time. Got it? He's older than you.'

'Four years four months older,' put in Jack. That was the precise difference, to the day, that we always pointed out.

'I'm cleverest.'

She snapped at me. 'Cleverer, Smart Alec, and you're not. You do as he says. Always.'

She was on delicate ground and she knew it. Although I was so much younger, I was a far better reader, coming top of my class regularly in most subjects and regarded as a very bright child, especially by myself. Jack, on the other hand, although no fool, was a very slow starter. He not only had the nuisance of a younger brother to deal with, he also had the humiliation of constantly being bettered by me in lessons and hearing me held up as an example to all. I, as a consequence, was pretty cocky. Getting me safely under Jack's wing must have been tricky for her.

'He's your big brother. You stay with him and do as he says. And you, Jack, you see that he does. All the time.'

Jack agreed, but the prospect of the pair of us being together the whole time, his albatross-little-brother round his neck, must have dismayed him as much as it did me. 'Can I bash him?'

She silenced my protests. 'There's no need for that but don't you stand any nonsense from him, Jack. And don't you dare leave him.'

I was indignant. 'I can look after myself.'

'All right, all right. You look after each other. How's that? You both look after each other.'

For Jack, the idea of being looked after by me, even partially, held no charm, but as he started to protest Mum threw in her final compromise. 'Just until you get to where you're going. Until you get there. Really there.'

'Where?'

There was no answer to that so she introduced her second point, her game. 'Now listen, both of you. Look what I've got here. It's a postcard. And it's in code. A secret code. Like the Secret Service. Only this is our code. Our own secret code. Read it, Jack.'

This was exciting stuff; the postcard was stamped and addressed to our parents. Jack started to stumble through it. ' "Dear Mum and Dad, Arr—arr—arrived safe and well. Ev—ev—every—" '

I snatched the postcard from him and rattled off, ' "Everything fine. Love, Jack and Terry." '

Mum was furious with me. 'Give that back at once. I told Jack to read it, not you. He's the older one, you do as he says. Always.'

'I don't see why—'

'*Always*.' The word was flung across the room at me, cutting through my disobedience, telling us both on a deeper level just how serious all this was. Jack completed the reading of the card, uninterrupted. There was a pause. Mum was getting hold of herself.

'But—what's the code?' Jack ventured nervously.

'When you get there,' she continued, 'you find

20

out the address of the place where they take you. And you write it on the card there.' She looked at us both. She had left a space. This was the really tricky bit. 'Here, Jack. Here's the pencil to write it with. You look after it. I'll put it in your case. And when you know the address—'

Jack cut across her. 'I'll give the pencil to Terry and he can write it in there.'

Mum was momentarily taken aback. She wasn't expecting such help. 'That's right, Jack. Good boy.' I didn't understand then why she gave him a hug that nearly stifled him when all he had done was to suggest the, to me, obvious solution. She continued to both of us, 'Then you post it at once. All right? Now listen, I've only got one card so you've *got* to stay together or I won't know where one of you is.' It was her final shot on the other subject that was eating her.

'But that's not a proper code.' We were disappointed.

'No. Now *this* is the code. Our secret. You know how to write kisses, don't you?' We agreed with 'earrgh', 'yuck' noises to brandish our distaste for such things. She waited for the ritual to subside. 'You put one kiss if it's horrible and I'll come straight there and bring you back home. D'you see? You put two kisses if it's all right. And three kisses if it's nice. Really nice. Then I'll know.'

In the anxiety and horror of this major crisis in her life—our lives—our mother, and perhaps our father too, had come up with something for them and us to cling to in the chaos. That night we slept soundly, perhaps dreaming of our code and the adventure to come.

21

She walked us under a canopy of barrage balloons to the 89 bus stop by the We Anchor In Hope pub at the foot of Shooters Hill. They were digging up the golf course to put in more anti-aircraft guns and searchlights. Welling, with the Thames and the docks a mile or two to the north, was on a direct route for bombers from the Continent heading for London. The water tower at the top of Shooters Hill was an outstanding landmark.

The narrow up-line platform of Welling station was packed with hundreds of excited, chattering, rampant, labelled children with their cases and their teachers and mothers. Four or five travellers on the down-line platform stood staring at the extraordinary sight opposite them. Teachers were ticking registers, two men were removing the station nameplates.

'Why're you doing that?' asked a pushy bigger boy.

The man who answered him fancied himself as a comedian. 'It's so the Germans won't know where they are when they get here.'

Our special train puffed round the bend into the station and the decibel-level rose sharply.

'It's an N-class,' Jack and I saw with intense disappointment. 'A manky old N. It hasn't even got a name.' We were clearly not as important as we thought, even though the N-class was a powerful 2-6-0, used for long-distance freight and passenger work. Suddenly we saw it was a corridor train and excitement again took over. Plenty of scope for fun: we could run from end to end of it, from compartment to compartment; lavatories to lock ourselves in; a guard's van to explore.

I don't remember seeing any tears on that platform but there must have been plenty. Jack and I stood at a window, waving and shouting at Mum, who stood in a crowd of waving, smiling mums. She mouthed, 'Don't forget the code,' as though we could have. She told me years later that she went home and sobbed. Like all the other mums, I expect. I still cannot think of her inventiveness and bravery, even now nearly seventy years later, without my eyes filling. Mum and Dad, with her (their?) secret code and his man-to-man confidences about our route and locomotives, ensured that Jack and I left home without a qualm. Perhaps even her success, seeing us shrug them off with such ease, gave another twist to the knife. We have all heard the stories of frightened, unhappy vackies being torn from their parents and shipped off to the unknown, but not Jack and me. As far as either of us can recall we just thought it was an adventure with his classmates and teachers and friends, although I had no difficulty in obeying Mum's instruction to stay close to my big brother. Perhaps I was more anxious than I realised. As one of the youngest I knew practically nobody there; I was the only representative of Eastcote Road Primary; my infant-schoolmates had been sent elsewhere, many of them with their mothers because they were too young to be separated. But Westwood Secondary School, situated too far from my home for me to know any of those children, was kept together, a gigantic school outing. In any case they were all, except the younger siblings like me, eleven or over—Jack had only just started there—so they were distant, godlike figures to a seven-year-old. None of that made any difference to my feelings; they were a seething, familiar-to-each-other crowd and I had Jack and was caught up in it all.

That manky old N-class puffed us off to our new lives and to my other childhood.

*   *   *

Our train left the usual route to Charing Cross at the Lewisham flyover, as Dad had forecast, and rumbled over the arched workshops, engine sheds (such excitement) and railway offices of south London. Jack and I disagreed about which side Dad had told us to look out of at Wandsworth Road. I looked left and he right. It seems that all south London was out there waving. Jack said he saw Dad in one place, I saw him in another. Dad later said he saw both of us, but all any bystander could see of that train was that it sprouted yelling, juvenile heads and waving arms from every aperture.

We passed from Victorian, industrial inner suburbs, via Clapham Junction, to Surbiton's twentieth-century semis with gardens, very like where we had come from but posher. Gathering pace we sped by the huge flower gardens of Sutton's seed factory near Woking. 'A Blaze of Colour' their seed packets used to proclaim, and it certainly was that day in high summer June. Then past Brookwood Cemetery, the London Necropolis, the largest cemetery in the country. It overwhelmed my imagination as so many graves sped past; all full, my morbid mind muttered to me. Jack and I knew that we were on the main

24

West of England line; out beyond the far reaches of electrification; on through Andover Junction, Basingstoke, Salisbury; through a level crossing at Wilton, I think, over streams, under bridges; a wait or two on sidings while more important war traffic roared past (what could be more important to a country than its future?). And everywhere there were people waving, always waving. The whole country knew of the evacuation.

A group of us gathered in a compartment to celebrate the birthday of June Burford, a girl of my age who I didn't know, another younger sibling. We sang 'Happy Birthday' and watched her unwrap presents brought by her sister, Pat, and two brothers, Derek and Peter. Then a cake was produced and we were all given a minute piece.

An age further on we pulled up at a major station with an unusually wide gap between the platforms: 'Exeter Central', it said. The Welling-station-nameboard-remover hadn't got there yet. There were some moments of excitement when a King Arthur-class engine pulled up opposite us across that gap, far enough away for us to have a good, full-length look at it: *Sir Bors*, the nearest we came to a named Southern Railway engine that day. What we did know was that the stop was only to change engines and pick up a little tank engine that would act as extra brakes as our train dived down the steep incline to Exeter St David's station and the main Great Western Railway line where we reversed direction. 'We're going home,' shouted some hopefuls. But no. The Southern Railway took the northern route round Dartmoor and the Great Western the southern; they arrive, bizarrely, in Plymouth from opposite directions, having come from the same starting point. The Southern Railway line (now gone) wandered through hilly Devon countryside, the Great Western Railway line ran (still runs) dramatically along the seashore at Dawlish. 'The sea,' yelled hundreds of excited voices in unison and our train heaved with excitement. It is a wonder it didn't tip over sideways as every child and teacher in it strained to get as close as possible to the waves breaking a few feet from us as we clanked along. Then Plymouth, the Royal Navy base at Devonport packed with grey, menacing warships, a slow rumble over Saltash Bridge, which had an armed sentry at each end, and we were told we were in Cornwall. Cornwall, it sounded all right: a wall of corn. But the first station we passed through was St Germans. Sainted Germans? Here? The next was Menheniot, which was incomprehensible. We crossed a viaduct, one of several, but this one was high over a deep little valley with a single-track railway far beneath us, and had a station at the end of it. We stopped there, the front of the train in a cutting, so steep were the contours. 'Liskeard', said the boards. We didn't even know how to say it. Was this a foreign country?

* * *

The afternoon sun shone down the length of the cutting, making bars of gold through the smoke and steam of our new engine, given to us at Exeter. A Great Western, a stranger, a Hall-class, but I forgot which one as we were led away and walked up the road in long crocodiles of twos, past curious

26

local people, to an assembly room where we were given a bun and squash. We were soon packed into buses which fanned out of Liskeard in all directions, breaking up Westwood Secondary School for good—well, anyway, for the duration.

Still going further west towards the sun, our bus followed another down a long winding hill past a vast railway viaduct, the biggest yet, with a mysterious, derelict one beside it: Moorswater. On, through strange folded countryside with a line of moors in the distance, to a school—granite and slate, small and bleak and Victorian—nothing like the brick-and-tile, airy, modern Westwood Secondary or Eastcote Road Primary in our modern pebble-dash estates. This one sat just outside the village, squat and solitary on a country road. All the buildings we had seen looked so old. Even the people waiting in the inadequate playground seemed older than our parents—the youngish marrieds who made up the adult population of our street at home.

The sixty or so of us were herded into the centre of the main schoolroom and the villagers crowded in after us and stood round the walls. What a scene, this auction of children with no money involved, almost medieval. The villagers slowly circled us and picked the most likely-looking. They used phrases strange to us in thick accents we could barely understand.

'Hallo, my beauty.'

'There y're, me 'andsome. Wha' be your name then?'

'Don' you worry none.'

'Us'll 'ave 'ee.'

' 'Er can come wi' I.'

'This one yere'll do we.'

Inhuman as it all could be judged now, I can think of no quicker, better way of dispersing us. I don't know if the other children felt fear or anxiety; some must have. I remember only curiosity. At least our new guardians were given some sort of choice in who was going to share their homes if the children were not. Not that anyone in authority in those days would have thought of consulting children about their welfare. One thing would seem to be sure: whoever was running things locally did a good job, because no brothers and sisters were split up that day. Some people took three or four children to keep families together. We knew this was so when we reassembled for school.

A female voice said to me, 'What about you, my pretty? D'you want to come wi' I?'

'I'm with my brother,' I said.

'Two of you, eh?'

'Yes, he's with me. We're staying together,' said Jack.

'Two boys is a bit much for we.' And the owner of the voice moved on.

A hand grabbed my hair, an action I always hated. There was quite a lot of it and it was fair.

'Yere. I'll have this one yere, little blondie,' said a female voice.

'Ow, that's my hair.'

'I know, boy. Could do with a cut, too.'

I cannot be quite sure about my first reaction to this person, older than my mother, who laid claim to me in such a way. Although the hand that had ruffled my hair had been less than gentle, she herself, looking down at me, did not look

28

intimidating. Her accent was different again, much easier to follow than much of what we were listening to.

'You've got to have my brother, too.'

'*Got* to?' Her eyebrows went up a little in surprise.

'Mum said we've got to stay together. She said so.'

'Did she now?'

'Yes, we're staying together,' said Jack, more firmly than he could possibly have felt.

'Are you now? And you're his brother, are you?'

'Yes. We're together.'

'Both of us,' I added, to clear up any possible misunderstanding.

She regarded us reflectively. 'That's right, then. If your mam said. How old are you, boys?'

We spoke eagerly and simultaneously. 'Eleven, nearly twelve.' 'Seven and a half.'

'And what are your names?'

Again we tumbled over one another. 'Jack.' 'Terry.'

'Well, you're a pair, aren't you?' she said and it sounded complimentary. 'I like boys, less trouble than girls. Girls, oh, *Duw*. Nimby-pimby, all tears and temper. Can you top 'n' tail?'

'We did that at our cousins' last year,' said Jack.

'Well, that's all right, then. You may be down in the front passage for a bit. We got two soldiers, see? Just for now. From Dunkirk. They'll soon be gone. Come on. Both of you. I like little blondies. Our family's dark, especially my son, Gwyn. He's in the Army, training in Wales.'

We left the vacky market. Outside she called out to someone. 'Here, over yere. We got two.'

29

'Oh *Duw*, girl. Can we fit 'em in?'

'We'll think of something. Come on, boys, quick, 'fore he changes his mind.'

The man, tiny, bald, tanned, rotund, like a hard rubber ball, had booked the solitary village taxi. He was much shorter than his wife, who was no great height. 'Here, boys, in you get, quick, 'fore someone else gets him. Ever ridden in a taxi?' He didn't wait for any possible reply. 'I hadn't when I was your age.'

And we were in the taxi with this odd couple, heading back up the lane, left on to the main road through the village, Dobwalls, where we— privileged in our vehicle—passed villagers walking home with their new vacky acquisitions.

Out into open country again, still towards the setting sun. The man sat in front with the driver, Jack and I behind with the woman. The man turned round. 'Now then, what's your names, boys?'

Once more neither of us waited for the other. 'Terry.' 'Jack,' we said in unison.

'And how old are you?'

'I'm nearly twelve,' said Jack as I said, 'I'm seven and a half.'

The man pretended to be confused. 'Have you thought of electing one of you to be chairman?'

This, in turn, confused us.

'Leave 'em alone, Jack,' said the woman, already protective.

He pointed at me. 'So, you're Jack.' He pointed at Jack, 'And you're Terry.' His finger stabbed at me again, 'And you're nearly twelve.' Back to Jack, 'And you're seven.'

We giggled. 'Don't be silly.'

He did it all again but correctly this time.

'That's right.'

'Well, thank God we got that straight.' His grin included us in his joke.

'Only seven, are you?' said the woman to me as though it were a wonder.

'Yes.' I was confident by now, too confident, and decided to identify myself. 'I'm the clever one.'

'Are you now?' said the man, his grin fading. He turned to Jack, 'And what are you?'

'I'm the older one.'

There was a silent moment during which he glanced at the woman, then looked from one to the other of us. 'Hmm,' was all he said.

She came in quickly. 'Well, that's funny, my husband is Jack too.'

Jack was amazed. 'Is your name really Jack?'

The man grinned again, instantly responding. 'Course it is. What d'you think? We're telling fibs?'

'Isn't that funny?' said Jack, pleased.

'We'll have to make sure we don't muddle you up, then, won't we?' said the woman.

'D'you think you can manage to tell the difference?' The man looked very concerned as we both laughed. 'Well, what's funny?' he asked. 'We look just the same, don't we?'

'He's younger 'n you,' I said.

'No, not much,' he replied.

'I've got hair,' said Jack, and this got a good laugh.

'Oh, cheeky, are we?' was the response.

'And you're redder than him and fatter. And you talk funny.' As always I went too far for my brother, though everyone else laughed.

'Please, I'm sorry. He didn't mean anything,'

Auntie Rose and Uncle Jack all dressed up in the Court

Jack said, embarrassed.

The woman was again all reassurance. 'That's all right, boy. He's only saying what he sees and hears. So. You call him Uncle Jack. And I'm Auntie Rose.'

The driver said something incomprehensible to the man.

He turned back to us. 'Hear that, boys? What he says about the vackies?'

'No,' we answered, mystified.

The driver half turned his head so that we could hear better and repeated whatever it was. We stared in silence.

'Is he speaking English?' I asked at last and earned a roar of laughter.

'Oh, ar, 'tis English all right,' he said. ' 'Tis Cornish. 'Tis proper English. We'll soon 'ave you talking it, don't you fret, my beauty.' Beauty, as he said it, came out as 'boody'.

'Not living with a Welshman, they won't,' said the man Jack. 'I'll tan it out of them.'

'Hark at them both,' chimed in the woman, defending us from the threatened assault. 'Double Dutch is all either of 'em can talk. You take no notice, boys.'

*   *   *

We swept past a farm with a huddle of outbuildings which grimly showed their backs to the weather and the outside world; they looked into shelter and pungent smells. We topped the brow of a hill with a lone oak tree growing from the hedge, not very tall but stark, only thinly veiled in June leaf, with all the branches blown one way like the fingers in a skinny hand pleading to the north-east for relief. We would soon learn to know intimately those prevalent (permanent so it sometimes seemed) south-westerlies that blew across Cornwall.

The man spoke. 'There we are. See? That's where we live. We're the end one. There.' We stared across a field at a terrace of Victorian cottages—more slate and granite. They looked tiny and grim. Seven of them, as it turned out. How could seven families live in so little space? 'That's Doublebois,' he said. He pronounced it 'Double-boys' as you might expect. He continued, 'Doublebois is French.' Now he tried a French pronunciation on it. 'Doobler-bwa'. That's French. It means two woods. Not two boys, two woods. Only we can say two boys now, isn't it?' And he laughed at his welcoming wit.

The taxi pulled up and we went through a little wrought-iron gate between a warehouse on the right and the row of seven cottages on our left. This area, we learned, was called the Court and all the back doors opened on to it. The Court was the common ground, the thoroughfare. We walked past a pump on the wall of the first cottage, down a narrow courtyard, past a large concrete rainwater tank halfway down on the right, joined to the back of the warehouse. A tap, set over a drain, jutted from this tank. All our washing water came from that, our drinking water from the pump. After this the Court widened a little with a small whitewashed bungalow on the right. We went to the end house of the terrace, which had a wooden wash-house beyond it and some hens in a wire-enclosed run on the right.

Neighbours looked out of doors at us. A woman said, 'Thought you was only getting one.'

'They was on special offer,' said our man.

'They looked too good to leave behind,' said his wife.

He grabbed my hair. 'This yere's Terry, the uppity one, and'—he patted Jack on the back—'Jack, my namesake, is the nice one.'

She was in quickly again. 'Leave them alone, Jack. They must be tired and hungry.' And she ushered us in.

We entered and stared in wonder at a shining black range with a cat curled beside it; at a canary in a cage; at a green velvet tablecloth; at a sideboard on which sat a little brass dustpan-and-crumbs brush; at a shapeless sofa; at oil lamps—no electricity here; at two First World War shells in their cases, over six inches tall, standing on either side of the clock on the mantelpiece. They took our excited attention, beating even the cat and the canary, with their soldered-on Army badges that had three feathers and 'Ich dien' on a scroll. The evening sun lit the room in nearly horizontal shafts full of dust; the room seemed packed with things and smelled of coal smoke and cooking.

But the glory came last: outside, past the hens in their run, right behind the wash-house, tucked down in a cutting and breathtakingly revealed, was the main London to Penzance railway line with Doublebois station practically below us, its goods yard and sidings a couple of hundred yards down-line beyond a road bridge at the far end of the station. In the short time before we went to bed—and even after—the rural silence of Doublebois was occasionally shattered as an express train

35

roared by a few yards below us, steam and smoke belching over the cottages. Local trains chuffed. In the mornings goods engines shunted and banged and clattered, shouts echoed, the arms of signals clanked from danger, to caution, to go, and bells in the signal box announced the up-train to Plymouth and the down to Truro and Falmouth. We two railway children couldn't have invented, couldn't have dreamed of arriving in such a place. Even our address, cumbersome but utterly satisfying, was: '7 Railway Cottages, Doublebois, Dobwalls, near Liskeard, Cornwall.'

CHAPTER THREE

The tiny front hall, where we were installed on a borrowed mattress on the floor, was a narrow passage that led to the front door, which was the 'back' door and never used. Everybody who entered Railway Cottages, except strangers, did so via the Court. They ignored the row of front gardens with their little gates, came down the Court and rapped on the back door which led straight into the back parlour or kitchen, the centre of the world in each cottage. If a stranger entered the gardens, walked the length of the terrace and banged on the front door, he was shouted at through the locks and bolts to come round the back, which was always open.

In the privacy of our mini-domain we stared at Mum's postcard by candlelight—a first for us— and considered our code. Jack held the pencil. 'How many kisses shall we put?'

I had no doubts. 'I vote three.'

'Hmm. I'm not sure.'

'Come on yere, you two. What's all this? Up-a-dando, into bed.'

Suddenly our new—surrogate—mother was with us. Jack slipped the postcard under his pillow—too late; she had seen but she said nothing. I think I remember her putting us to bed that first night, at once making us feel at home, secure. But perhaps my memory is playing me false and I am running many bedtimes into one because sometimes we are in the hall on the floor (where we were occasionally put when visitors stayed) and sometimes we are upstairs in what became our room. However, whichever place it was, there was always her warmth, her smiling good humour, her tact with two children who were not her own, just the presence of her. 'Come on, then. Who's going at which end?'

I grabbed the corner to snuggle into. But Jack was doubtful.

'Will there be enough air for him in the corner? You see . . .' He trailed off unhappily. 'He won't tell you, but—'

'Oh no,' I breathed. He was splitting on me.

'I must.'

'Must what, boy?'

'He gets asthma.'

'I don't. Not much.'

'All right, all right, young 'un. I won't tell anyone.' She turned to Jack and treated his concern with careful respect. 'Now listen, you—Jack. We can't open the front door, we'll have God knows what animals and creepy-crawlies in yere, but we'll leave the door to the front room open;

there'll be lots of air and he'll be able to breathe there in the corner, you take my word. I know 'bout asthma. Is that all right?'

'Yes, thank you, Mrs Phillips.'

'Did your mam tell you to see about the air?'

'No, I thought of it myself.'

'Did you now? You're a fine boy. Now into bed, go on. No. Wait a minute. Do you say your prayers at night?'

We stared.

'All right, I'll say a prayer for both of you. In you get. My Jack's a heathen, too. Look, boys, if you want to go outside during the night you got this yere. D'you see?' She showed us a flowered jerry, hidden under a cloth.

We knew what a jerry was, of course, but her phraseology confused us. 'Why should we go outside?' asked two boys brought up in modern, plumbed Welling.

'To go down the garden, of course. To the privy.'

'Oh, yes. Outside. Sorry, Mrs Phillips.' We had already used the odorous, unattractive privies, one feature of our life in Cornwall that I remember without affection. There were two cubicles, each a wooden two-seater, making four places in all. Though four people sitting there simultaneously doesn't bear thinking about.

'Auntie Rose, I said you call me. Right?'

'But you're not our auntie. Our auntie's in Portslade.'

'No, no, I'm not. You're right. You call me Auntie Rose when you want to, is it?'

I wriggled down into the soft feather mattress we were to sleep on. 'Cor, it's ever so nice in here.'

'There. Look at you. As snug as bugs in a rug.'

'What?'

'Tha's what we say. As snug as a bug in a rug. Only there's two bugs in my rug.'

'I'm not a bug,' said Jack, enjoying himself.

'He's a bugger sometimes.'

Her face momentarily showed that I had gone too far.

Jack was in at once. 'I'm sorry, Mrs—um—he didn't mean to say that. He's just stupid sometimes.'

'I'm not. You are.'

'Well, he's young, isn't he? When he gets to your age he'll know better. Now I'm going to put out the candle, if you're ready?'

'Could you leave it, please?'

'Don't you like the dark?'

'No, it's not that. We got to—um—do something.'

'It's bedtime now.'

'We got to send a card to Mum and Dad.'

'This one?' She had moved round, sat on the floor and satisfied her curiosity about what we had been up to when she came in by producing the postcard from under the pillow.

We were dismayed. 'Yes.'

'Is that your writing? It's very grown-up.'

'No, it's Mum's.'

'Well, she's already written the card.'

'We got to put your address on it.'

'Well, you've done it, haven't you? Yes, that's more like your writing. That's not how you spell Liskeard. I'll do you another card in the morning. A nice new one with a picture. How's that?'

'No, no. We got to put something else on.'

39

'What's that?'

She was met with silence.

'Well?' she asked gently.

'Er—kisses.'

'All right, then. We can do that, too, in the morning.'

'*We* want to do it.'

'By ourselves.'

She stared at us, reading something special and prepared to give us our heads now that she knew that we were up to no mischief. When she spoke again her voice was even more gentle, more reassuring than she had sounded so far. 'All right, then. You do it by yourselves, is it? That's right. You got something to write with?'

'Yes. Here. A pencil.'

'All right, then. I'll leave the candle lit and then come back again and watch you put it out the right way. We don't want a fire, do we? Your mam wouldn't like that.' And she left us.

'How many kisses?'

'I vote three.' I had no doubts.

'Perhaps we should take one off cos we're on the floor, not even a bed.' Jack continued to take his older-brother responsibilities seriously.

'I don't care.'

'There's no taps in the house.'

'It's triffic here. Trains and everything.'

I am sure he felt the same as I did but wanted to be sure. 'What about no electricity?'

'I don't care.'

'And no lavatory.' It was his last try.

I went on stubbornly, 'I don't care.'

He relaxed. 'Me neither.' At last he said what we were both feeling. 'It's like being on holiday

40

only there's no sea.'

'We could put four,' I said. 'The more we put, the happier Mum and Dad will be.'

'D'you think so?'

'Yeah.'

*   *   *

We ringed the card with kisses and posted it next morning.

CHAPTER FOUR

When Jack and I ringed that card with kisses there was an unintended symbolism: Jack and I were ringed with love, though we didn't know it and would have been embarrassed to have used such words.

Our foster-parents Rose and Jack Phillips were Auntie Rose and Uncle Jack to everybody in Doublebois. This was extraordinary: they were not Cornish; they had only lived in the tightly knit little hamlet for ten or fifteen years (a blink in rural timescales); he was neither church nor chapel, though she occasionally went to church and—even more occasionally—dragged him along. Yet even the ancient Mrs Moore next door and Granny Peters, two doors up the Court, a whole generation older than them, always called them in the broadest Cornish Ahn'ee Rose and Uncle Jack. It was clearly some sort of tribute to their characters. He was a South Wales miner turned platelayer on the Great Western Railway. Their own two sons and one daughter were grown-up. Uncle Jack had been in the trenches in the First World War, in the Royal Welch Fusiliers, involved in some very heavy fighting. He had been invalided out with shrapnel wounds. Our father had been too young to be conscripted for the First World War and was just too old for this one, while Jack and I were—as yet—too young. We were a lucky family. But Uncle Jack and his sons fell precisely into the wrong age groups.

Two others who were in the wrong age group were a pair of soldiers, privates, who were the reason for Jack and me having to top 'n' tail for a few nights on the mattress in the hall. They were up in the back, or I should say front, bedroom and were direct from Dunkirk, stationed in the grounds of Doublebois House, a large Victorian mansion which stood in its own substantial wooded grounds with two gated entrances just down and across the road from Railway Cottages. It had been turned into an Army camp, complete with Nissen huts up the twin drives to the big house, where the officers were. When we arrived, immediately after the Army's retreat from France, the whole place was overflowing. Soldiers were billeted anywhere and everywhere. I don't know how the local people had found room for us vackies.

One of our two soldiers was bright and nervous, the other had undergone some sort of shock and just sat staring into space the whole time he was there. The bright one smoked a lot and winked at Jack and me about his companion, making light of something that clearly concerned him. He tended his comrade's every need, taking him out to the wash-house to shave him and leading him to the outside privy. I felt simultaneously grown-up to be taken into his confidence and embarrassed about an adult taking so much trouble to reassure us boys. We watched them with childhood's detached curiosity.

I can see Auntie Rose's concerned, unhappy face when she looked at the benumbed soldier and offered him food and drink. And, even more, Uncle Jack's quiet, respectful movements when he entered his own house with this damaged man in it. He had been there and understood. Then, quite soon and suddenly, they were gone in a roar of army lorries, and Jack and I shared the front bedroom, which was the back bedroom and looked down the gardens, over the outdoor privies behind their discreet hedges, across a cornfield, the railway line in full view on the right as it rose out of the cutting and curved away towards Liskeard, Plymouth and England, where we had come from. Yes, with Welsh foster parents in Cornwall and sentries guarding Saltash Bridge, we soon learned that the River Tamar was a frontier.

*   *   *

The hamlet of Doublebois had four local children; to these were added eight vackies, four from Welling—Jack and me, and Harold and Alan Packham, billeted rather grandly across the main road in the solid detached house of the district nurse, Miss Laity—and four from Plymouth: the three Plummer boys, Peter, Eric and Ken, and one girl, Elsie Plummer, a cousin of some sort, who didn't live with the rest of the Plummers but was

Me, one week after arriving in Cornwall

billeted on Miss Polmanor, the Doublebois Wesleyan zealot. More later of this unhappy pairing.

A few months later, when the summery Battle of Britain, fought in daylight over the Kent and Sussex skies of our former home, evolved into the nightly, autumnal Blitz on London, another vacky joined us: five-year-old Teddy came to 3 Railway Cottages with his mother and baby sister.

On our first morning the four Welling vackies met the four locals—Jimmy Peters and the three Bunney children—in a smallish triangle of land euphemistically known locally as the Park. The Park was at the crossroads in Doublebois. This was a five-road crossroads consisting of the main road running east to west, a lane going north to Bodmin Moor or south to Lostwithiel, and Station Approach sloping down to the up-platform and ticket office. When you add to that the two sentried entrances to Doublebois House and the main railway line running down the valley you have a veritable rural Piccadilly. But little stirred there until a train stopped or the army was on the move.

The Park had several magnificent beech trees, especially one right on the corner from which you could see everything in Doublebois: all of the dozen or so houses, the station, over to the Bunneys' farm, the goods sidings with Blamey and Morgan's mill, especially the trains panting up the long gradient from the west into the station. We were soon up it day in and day out.

That tree, our tree, also commanded an astonishing view: the Fowey Valley, almost as heart-stopping as the first sight of the sea on

45

summer holiday. The main road plunged down on one side of the valley past a quarry into woods; the railway snaked parallel along the other side on a thrilling succession of bridges and viaducts; between them initially was a field, the Rabbit Field, we learned, beyond which the tops of trees waved and swayed into the hazy distance, beckoning magically and majestically. We all hung from the branches of this tree. Jack voiced the shared, aching longings of the four vackies.

'Let's go down the woods.'

There was a silence while the locals stared at us. Then in broad Cornish from David Bunney, 'Wha' frr?'

It was our turn to stare at them. 'What for?'

'Yeah. Wha' frr?'

'To play.'

'Play wha'?'

'Just play.'

'Wha's wrong wi' yere?'

We stared at the crossroads beneath us and away out over the enchanted valley. *'Can't you see?' 'Are you blind?'* There lay adventures, endless woods, a rushing river, fish to catch, streams to dam, paths, tracks, the quarry to climb, creatures and things we hadn't heard of. What for?

The locals drifted away as we vackies charged down the Rabbit Field kicking the tops off thistles and on into the dappled gloom of our vast new empty playground.

*　　　*　　　*

A day or so after I got to Doublebois I was playing with Alan Packham down on Station Approach by the entrance to the up-line. We were throwing the little stones that had worked loose from the tarmac at each other. There was no animosity in this. I threw a handful and one made a tiny hole in the top-left-hand pane of the frosted-glass window of the booking office. I tried to claim it was Alan's fault because he had been in front of the window and ducked when I threw. My pleas fell on deaf ears. The matter was reported to Auntie Rose and Uncle Jack. I was ashamed to be in their bad books so quickly. They sent me to apologise to Mr Rawlings, the stationmaster, and to offer to pay for the damage (with what, God knows). He gave me a lecture about shortages of glass—the panes had wire mesh in them to strengthen them, not very effective against vackies with stones—and told me the pane couldn't be replaced. It stayed unmended for the duration, rebuking me every time I went down Station Approach. The ticket clerk sat behind it when on duty and I always wondered if he got a stiff neck from the draught when it was cold. It finally had some paper stuffed into it. The incident also affected my relationship with the stationmaster, who was an imposing figure anyway. I decided that he had me marked out as a bad lot and I avoided him when I could. I found his gaze intimidating the whole time I was in Doublebois. I have no idea what he really thought of me, if anything.

*   *   *

Just a day or two after that incident I was with some others up our beech tree: vackies and Doublebois children. We had soon found we had

47

enough interests in common to make friends in spite of what we saw as their lack of gumption. School was in shifts. There was nowhere to put all the children at once so some of us were off that afternoon watching army lorries going in and out of the camp. Everything to do with the army fascinated all of us. We asked the guards on the entrances if we could touch their rifles and generally made nuisances of ourselves. In the first nervous aftermath of Dunkirk we were told to buzz off in no uncertain terms, but as things calmed down we were tolerated and then even welcomed by some, perhaps missing their own kids, so that the army camp became another adventure playground made even more alluring by the element of danger involved in dodging guards and officers.

We watched a train from Plymouth pull into the station. A Hall-class engine was drawing it. Jimmy Peters, son of another platelayer, the sub-ganger in Uncle Jack's gang, didn't even need to watch. He could identify a few of the individual engines that regularly drew our trains just by their sound; something I quickly learned from him. One or two people strode up Station Approach. I stared in wonder. My mother—my mother, lugging a heavy suitcase—was actually trudging up from the station towards me. She had received our card all right but had turned up anyway. I did not rush to greet her; instead, I turned and raced up the road, past the stationmaster's house, past Jimmy Peters' house, into the Court, down it and breathlessly indoors.

'Auntie Rose, Auntie Rose, Mum's here. My mum's here. She's outside,' I gulped, excited beyond belief. I didn't see her reaction, though she must have been flustered, because having delivered the news I turned and ran straight back to Mum.

My mother has often since reminded me of that moment. Her blue-eyed boy recognised her, turned and ran away. Whatever was wrong with him? It clearly upset her. She said that all sorts of anxieties took over in those few minutes before I came back. Nothing was wrong at all, of course. I had simply run to tell Auntie Rose. Had Auntie Rose become, in under a week, the first person in my life to share such things with, leaving my mother in the road outside?

I have no real idea of how Auntie Rose and Mum got on in that first meeting but it must have been well. When amoral, raffish Brighton met a South Wales mining village there was plenty of room for misunderstanding, to say nothing of the generation and class divides. Mum, with her good looks and classic lines to her face, always looked classier than we actually were. I don't know what Auntie Rose thought of Mum but Mum must have trusted Auntie Rose immediately because she told her about the kisses code and our judgement of her. I hope it gave Auntie Rose the pleasure she deserved.

As they settled down over tea, I was driven out. They wanted to talk about us. I went down the main road into the valley, to the bridge over the River Fowey. It was a place of infinite attraction for me all the time I was in Cornwall. There was a pool under the bridge where there were always trout and, seasonally, sea trout. There were rapids below the pool.

I scrambled down a path from the road to a

49

*My mother's favourite photo of herself taken on
holiday after the war*

little piece of bank that jutted into the river just above the rapids. There were magical things to be seen, including two sorts of dragonflies: the smaller, common green ones, really damsel flies, I think, and the larger ones with yellow and black hoops. One of these flew out in front of me and I looked up from my study of the water and reached out to it, not to catch it, I think, just to touch it. Into the river I went and found myself clinging to the bank, up to my chest, shocked, freezing cold and shouting with all my might as the current pulled at me. When I had left the road I had noticed one of Uncle Jack's mates from the platelayers' gang going home. He was pushing his bike up the long hill to Doublebois. Within moments I saw him above me, jumping the wall by the road and slithering swiftly down the steep path to where I was. We all marvelled later at how he stopped himself without going in, because—as he said—that's what he thought he would have to do. He lugged me out, sat me on his bike and pushed me up the hill. Mum's and Auntie Rose's tea was broken up with the arrival of Uncle Jack's grinning workmate and one dripping, shivering vacky.

' 'Ee got a proper voice on 'im,' said the platelayer. 'I 'eard 'ee all right. Good job I was there. 'Ee'd 'a' been gone. Swept away.'

*   *   *

The platelayer's assessment of my situation may have been a trifle lurid but Mum said that she constantly worried that her two sons would never survive the war. My rescue from drowning within an hour of her arrival did nothing to reassure her.

51

London was unthinkable and the country too unpredictable for her.

But for Jack and me the world was secure; the war was an exciting but unthreatening event; Cornwall was an adventure, with Auntie Rose and Uncle Jack simply there, our 'other parents', taken for granted. That was their achievement. We soon learned that it was Uncle Jack who was colourful, the one who entertained us or riveted us with his actions, stories and views of the world that we were just beginning to discover. But his life, their marriage—and now our lives—were based on the solid foundation of Auntie Rose. She was generally self-effacing, firm and—like him—utterly reliable. Going home to her was in no time as natural as going home to Mum. I believe in retrospect that a great part of the self-confidence of these two people and their partnership was that they each knew who they were. They were part of the working-class culture they came from and embodied. And 'working class' was exactly the right definition for them. They knew their jobs and did them, earning their rest as fully paid-up members of the hard-work union. They had their own natural courtesy to each other. Their lives were full of unmentioned demarcation lines and no-go areas that both understood and observed. The unselfconscious way they gave ground or claimed it between themselves was over my head, lost on me at that time, part of the scenery. Each knew their own domain, respected the other's boundaries and didn't stray over them. Well, anyway, Auntie Rose didn't, and when Uncle Jack did he was put smartly in his place. Something he always meekly accepted without ever losing his masculinity. Uncle Jack had the sense to realise his good fortune in marrying such a woman, and Auntie Rose was equally blessed. She never wanted anything other than their welfare—and now ours. If that is not a description of a love match then I don't know what is. But the word love seems too insubstantial to describe the deep roots, the thick foliage, the hard-wearing warp and weft of their union.

After Mum's first visit they were given express permission—if they needed it—to treat us exactly like their own children and punish us when we deserved it. I can think of no better expression of the trust Mum had in them from the word go. And I can still see Auntie Rose's slightly enquiring smile when we pleased her and still feel the warmth of her body when she held me; and her hands, so much more roughened than my mother's, but just as gentle.

She would grumble when she hadn't slept well. 'Oh *Duw*, I feel like a stewed owl,' and she had a saying which she used on afternoons when she wanted a nap—no amount of mockery from us would make her abandon it—'I'm just going upstairs to throw myself down.'

But Auntie Rose was not just a cuddly mum-figure. We had to live by her standards, and it was not a good idea to forget or flout them. She once gave me a lesson that bypassed the mind, etched itself into me and is still there. It was a while later; I was, perhaps eight or nine. Her daughter-in-law, Ethel, wife of older son Len, was staying. The three of us went for a walk up the lane to St Cleer and the moor; each of us had a jam-jar to search for wild strawberries. There weren't many but I persevered and after much effort had a miserable half-jarful while Auntie Rose and Ethel picked few. They preferred to natter. When we were back home I poured mine on my plate at teatime and planned which of the best ones to save till last.

Auntie Rose looked across the table at me. 'You've got your strawberries there, then, have you, boy?'

'Yes,' I answered, not sure what was wrong.

'Aren't you going to offer them round, then? We got a guest.'

I flushed till the hair rose on my neck, aware of my gracelessness but also of the injustice. 'But you two didn't bother. I mean—I picked these while you were talk—and—'

'Greed I'm bringing up yere, is it? What if I only gave you the food you got yourself?'

'I—sorry—I—er. Would you like some?' I offered my plate to Ethel.

'No, thank you, Terry,' she said.

'Would you, Uncle Jack?'

Uncle Jack was equally unhelpful. 'No, thanks, boy.'

I turned to my nemesis. 'Auntie Rose, would you like some?'

She hadn't finished. 'No, you do have 'em, boy. You obviously need 'em most.'

The chickens ate the wild strawberries.

*   *   *

And there was Uncle Jack, with his ferocious, secret scowls, sudden broad grins and his brusque delivery. In spite of these characteristics—or perhaps because of them—he was far less

54

Jack on parapet of River Fowey bridge

intimidating than Auntie Rose could be when she thought it necessary. One day he caught Jack and Ken Plummer trying to smoke down the garden beyond the privies. I was allowed to watch but not join in and waste the precious single Player's Weight (one genteel, feminine step above the inevitable working man's Woodbine) that Ken had stolen from his mother's packet. Uncle Jack didn't ask us where the cigarette had come from; he knew that unless it was one of his the answer would only involve his having to report the theft to someone else and compound the matter. He regarded us seriously and spoke man to man. 'You don't want to smoke, boys. It'll stunt your growth.' This was what we were all told at that time but Uncle Jack carried the evidence about with him. 'I smoked when I was your age and look what happened to me.' As he drew himself up to his full five foot nothing his eyes twinkled in self-mockery and his rebuke floated away like exhaled smoke. To redeem the seriousness of the moment he urged Ken and Jack to take a full drag and inhale. Of course they both choked and he strode away knowing that he had done all he could to discourage the unstoppable habit.

Uncle Jack's 'If I was your father, I'd—' was the start to many a threat that held few terrors for Jack or me. 'Bloody Cornish,' he would say without rancour. 'God-bothering, Bible-punching Tories.' And then the sentence that was applied to anyone who had a moan about something or who displeased him in some way, 'Send 'em down the mines for a bit, then they'd know they were born.'

I wondered what Tories were and why they punched Bibles. Jack explained. 'It's just an

56

expression. They don't actually punch them. I think they just bang them down hard in church or chapel. I've seen them do it with hymn books. And cowboys do it in the pictures too. They talk about punching cattle but they never do; they just punch each other.' I stared at a cow in a field and imagined punching its massive forehead, wringing my fist in agony as a result.

'Bloody Churchill.' This was another of Uncle Jack's remarks that seized our shocked attention. 'He sent the troops in against us at Tonypandy.' 'Us' were his beloved South Wales miners, on strike for a living wage. His complaint, I later learned to my dismay, was in reference to the notorious government reaction to that strike in 1910 when Churchill was Home Secretary.

'Nye Bevan, there's your man. On the Opposition benches all by himself. Attlee, Morrison, Bevin, they're all in the Government. Part of it. Sold out.' The Labour Party, who he had voted for all his life, had united with the arch-Conservative Churchill to form a coalition government and win the war. They earned only Uncle Jack's contempt. Nye Bevan, Uncle Jack's Welsh, left-wing idol, was the man who stood out virtually alone against the war and coalition (though he rejoined his colleagues in the Labour government that swept to power in the aftermath to found the National Health Service).

Of course, even though we were children of a couple who were also Labour—neither had any time for the Establishment, Dad because of his trade-union background and Mum because of her suffragette, musical family—the politics was over my head at first, but I learned.

'Ernie Bevin . . .' Uncle Jack rumbled to a bitter, thoughtful silence.

We knew of Bevin, a major trade-union figure, now Minister of Labour, former official of the Dockers Union, powerful and popular in our eyes, subsequently Foreign Secretary in Attlee's post-war government. Whatever was coming next? 'Yes? What about him?'

'He tried to call a general strike of all the British unions and the German ones to stop the first lot in 1914. They called him a traitor. Now he's one of them. Urging us all to join up and fight. Huh. Bevin Boys.' (Young men who couldn't or wouldn't be conscripted into the army were often directed down the mines to help the war effort under Bevin's rule, known as Bevin Boys.)

There were the one-sided arguments that Uncle Jack had with the BBC Home Service newsreaders.

'It's no good, Jack, he can't year you and the boys and me aren't listening,' Auntie Rose would interject.

But we were. It was from these outbursts that Jack and I learned the political and religious geography of our world. I found these attacks on people I had barely heard of, but had been conditioned to hold in esteem, thrilling and subversive. They gave us the references that influenced our lifelong political thinking. One day I asked Uncle Jack why he came to Cornwall if he didn't like it. 'Work, boy, work. No work there in the Valleys. Come with the Great Western, didn't I? The Company.' This word was spat out in a way that questioned my hitherto benevolent view of all things railway. 'Got the house an' all. Tied. Huh.

58

Tied. Like our lives.' Of course I didn't then understand all that was behind that, but as comprehension grew so there was a growing awareness of how the world about me worked differently for different people.

In spite of these sentiments, Uncle Jack seemed to like living in Cornwall. I cannot believe that working on the glorious three and a half miles of track that wound westward down the Fowey Valley from Doublebois and was his gang's stretch wasn't infinitely preferable to any coal mine, no matter how strong the camaraderie down there. I think he must have been painfully split between his leftist, internationalist, socialist ideals and his patriotism, as were so many. He certainly supported the war effort, going into the underused front room to listen, rapt, to Churchill's speeches on the wireless, which ran from great acid batteries that needed frequent changing and charging. And he went drinking on Saturday nights with his allegedly Tory, church-or-chapel Cornish workmates, singing his way home from a pub in Liskeard—for Dobwalls was dry, the Wesleyans had seen to that. 'Bloody chapel. Bloody hypocrites,' Uncle Jack used to growl, but, like Dad, he was no great drinker, he just liked to have something to beat the Methodists with.

When he went with his workmates to Liskeard for a drink on a Saturday they had to be on the last down-train or it was a four-mile walk home. They would pile out of it, go to the rear end (our end) of the down-platform, cross the line as the train left to continue its way west, greet the signalman in his box just below us, scramble up the narrow, steep footpath that climbed up the cutting between the

59

nettles and bushes, slip through the wire behind the wash-house and there they were, at the end of the Court. I remember one warm, magical night when they stopped at the top of the footpath to relieve themselves. They must have been a bit tight or noisy, probably singing, because Jack and I were awake and quickly up.

They were hissed at by Auntie Rose at the back door. 'Sssh, Jack. Everyone'll year. All up the Court.'

'I should hope so. Half of 'em are out yere with me,' was Uncle Jack's reply, half smothered in his own and others' giggles. 'Four miles to wet your whistle.' He raised his voice to complain to the world. 'It's bloody antediluvian. Bloody Methodists. Bloody Cornwall.'

'Oh-ho-ho. Plenty of time for all that in the morning. Bed now. Shall I wake you for morning service, is it?' Auntie Rose demonstrated her control of the situation with a shaft that brought grins from the others.

Uncle Jack's 'I'll bloody kill you if you do' had no more threat for Auntie Rose than did his other, more sober, threats to Jack and me.

'You couldn't kill a dozy fly with a frying pan. Come on, up to bed. You'll wake the boys.'

'It's all right, Auntie Rose. We're awake.' We were already down at the back door.

'Oh *Duw*. Back inside, you two, before you catch your deaths.'

'Want to splash your boots, boys?' was the far more alluring suggestion from Uncle Jack.

'Yes, yes, I'm bursting, I'm dying to.' And we two whippets were past Auntie Rose and through the wires to join him and splash anything we could manage. We thought we were men indeed to stand in such a row, barefoot on an enchanted summer Saturday night, as the last train's sounds echoed over the Fowey Valley and left the dozen or so houses of Doublebois to silence.

CHAPTER FIVE

We went to school in the village of Dobwalls, a good mile away, east along the A38 main road. Both schools, vackies' and village kids', were at the far end, to add to the yardage. We Doublebois children walked there and back every school day for the three years I was there, in all weathers, mostly wet it seems now. Nothing was thought of this; there were other children just as far-flung making their way to school from different directions. Though I recall that coming home sometimes seemed to be endless. To breast the last rise with the lone oak tree at the top, bent and stunted, growing only one way in the wind, and to see Railway Cottages, with ours on the end, was always welcome. I don't think there was a single fat child in Doublebois—or Dobwalls for that matter—and few, if any, adults. Wartime rationing had little or nothing to do with it: the greedy could always find something to eat in the country. It was simply that whatever we put into our mouths was burned away in constant physical activity.

In Dobwalls village the vackies and the village children took one look at each other and it was instant war. It wasn't, as far as I remember, that we hated each other, but simply that we regarded

61

Vacky boys soon after arrival—no wonder we intimidated the village kids. I am seated front left, I think

them with contempt, and they resented the pushy newcomers. Perhaps it started from the very first meetings. They only had to open their mouths to be objects of ridicule to us. Perhaps they were trying to be friendly. 'Whirr be you fram, then?' was greeted with suppressed giggles and 'You talk funny'.

'No, us don't. You do.'

We all stared at each other.

'Wha' be you staring at, then?'

And the usual knowing answer. 'Don't know, it ain't got a label.'

'What be you looking so glum for?'

'There's nothing to do here,' answered the vackies. (A view not shared by us at Doublebois. We had the station and goods yard, flour mill and stock pens, big house, Army camp, the valley, the woods and the river. But when in Dobwalls we showed solidarity without even thinking about it.) 'No Woolworth's, no pictures, nothing.'

'Well, go home, then. Nobody asked you to come.'

'We can't. Bombing.'

'There bain't no bombing' (and there wasn't yet). 'I reckon 'tis cos your mothers don't want you.'

'You haven't even got pavements. It's a dump.'

'No, 'tisn't, 'tis our village.'

One vacky thought of a great joke. 'Oh, 'tis it?' All the vackies laughed. 'Well, you can keep it.'

Stung, the village kids' answer was, 'Townies. Slum kids'.

'Turnips. Yokels. Clodhoppers.'

We twelve Doublebois children would walk to school together quite happily but, when we got to the village, we separated, without conscious effort, into vackies and village kids.

Dobwalls straggled in an undistinguished way for more than half a mile along the main A38. There were a few houses down side lanes and that was more or less it; some few hundred inhabitants. The first building we came to at our end was the post-and-telegraph office, on the left, set back from the road, strangely in a bungalow with a long garden path. Then the Lostwithiel road forked into ours and we were in the village, with Ede's shop on the right and Rowe's garage facing it on the left. Three lanes joined the main road as it forked, one prong leading back to Doublebois and Bodmin and the other diving under the railway line to East Taphouse and Lostwithiel. This six-pronged junction, as complex as ours in Doublebois, had no more traffic than we did. We split up as we passed the shop, walked on past the main drinking-water tap at the bottom of a little hill and up the other side past St Peter's, the tiny Anglican church. At the far end, the village kids turned right and had the pleasure of going past the forge of Mr Uglow, the blacksmith, where horses sometimes stamped uneasily, aware of the burning smells from within, and all sorts of exciting things could be happening, before continuing a little way down the Duloe road to their school. The vackies turned left into the Methodist graveyard, where—not surprisingly—nothing ever happened unless we made it. Our main classroom was in the chapel; our infants' class, my class, was behind the graveyard in a wooden building with a corrugated-iron roof misnamed the Hall; our playground was the consecrated churchyard, hide-and-seek

64

between the slabs of slate. We were forbidden to leave the churchyard during the day and they were not allowed out of their school playground. This, of course, led to the more adventurous escaping to taunt the other lot over their wall and then run away. After school there would be more taunts and scuffles. Once we Doublebois lot had got clear of the village we joined up and continued on our amicable way home.

The vackies had one song, favourite among the many that were used, sung to the tune of 'A Gordon For Me':

> The turnips are thick, the turnips are dumb;
> They use stinging nettles for wiping their bum.
> They eat mangel-wurzels and live in a shed;
> They're dotty and spotty and soft in the head.

The village kids' song, to the tune of 'Blow Away The Morning Dew', had, in my view even then, more style. I think I liked the tune better:

> They come down yere from London so swanky
>   and stuck up;
> They challenge us to take them on and say they'll
>   duff us up.
> So we'll blow away them vacky kids to kingdom
>   come;
> We'll blow away them smarty-pants and kick
>   them up the bum.

Perhaps the last five words let it down. The tunes, of course, we all knew well from school.

Efforts were made to improve relations. They were futile.

Some well-meaning person suggested a cricket match: we walloped them. A football match followed: the score was, believe it or not, vackies thirty-odd, village kids nil. Our contempt for them was confirmed. Westwood Secondary School—no great shakes academically, consisting almost entirely of grammar- and technical-school rejects—was streets ahead of Dobwalls village school. We younger brothers and sisters soon saw that we were equally superior to their infants. As we came from the suburbs with woods and greenery, even their strengths, the mysteries of the countryside, were partly known by us, though we had much to learn. When it came to street wisdom the gap was unbridgeable. They didn't seem to have heard of knock-down-ginger or scrumping. If they wanted an apple they either asked or took one. Or of stealing from Woolworth's—for obvious reasons that we vackies made no allowances for, although it soon became apparent to even the most hardened of us that you couldn't possibly steal from Ede's, the village shop, not because it was too dangerous but because it was too personal. Unthinkable to take things from Mr Ede and his brother. The anonymity needed for petty crime was gone.

We arranged our own private group fights—more confrontation and insults than violence—in the dinner break and returned to our separate classes late and dishevelled, to get our knuckles rapped with a ruler—more painful than the fights. And our leader, Frank Emmett, and their leader, Sam Finch, fought each other in single combat to wild cheers and a disputed result.

The whole village divided. Those with their own

children and many others regarded the vackies as a pestilence to be endured or resisted. But there were those who suddenly found themselves with new families: energetic, bright children who won their hearts and brought a new vitality to their village, trebling the under-fourteen population. And, of course, there must have been the unfortunate misfits, vackies who were too difficult to manage for one reason or another and villagers who just couldn't handle the children dumped on them. But, although the stories of cruelty and abuse abound and resound even now, I remember none among my fellows who was mistreated. Though there was one little boy in Junior Vackies who often wet himself, so at least one of us was unhappy. When he did it, someone would hold up their hand and say, 'Please, Miss. Dozmary Pool.' (A famous stretch of water on Bodmin Moor.) And he became the humiliated centre of stifled mirth as Mrs Langdon patiently cleaned him and the floor up. I remember no sign of sympathy from us young savages and he was one of those who soon went home.

Prominent among the pro-vackies faction was the Reverend Clifford Buckroyd, the Wesleyan Methodist Minister, a pleasant, good-looking, fortyish man (my mother told me years later that every time she visited us she always fancied him, which surprised me as much as an adult as it would have done had she told me at the time—he was a *minister* for goodness sake) who worked hard to make us vackies feel at home and the village accept us. He was a popular man and lives clearly in my memory. If personality had dictated where people worshipped, his chapel would have been overflowing and the Anglican church empty. I can barely remember its vicar, the Reverend R. O. Oatey, though I attended it for three years, taken there by Auntie Rose. But denominations and places of worship were ingrained, only marginally decided by such ephemeral factors.

*   *   *

There was one Wesleyan Methodist woman, the anti-vacky Miss Polmanor, the one on whom Elsie Plummer had the misfortune to be billeted, who seemed to personify all the traits of uptight bigoted Christianity that made Uncle Jack so angry. It abounded in the country in those days. When I say country I don't just mean countryside, I mean the whole country. No one had a monopoly on it. Miss Polmanor lived in one of a pair of houses some yards from the Court, up the road towards Dobwalls. But her religious convictions meant that there was more to her than mere narrow-mindedness, as I learned in due course. She was harder on herself than on anyone. She seemed to make her own life something to be endured rather than enjoyed. There was, no matter what Uncle Jack might have thought or said, not the faintest whiff of hypocrisy in her. Whatever she demanded of people she first drew from herself. I became, soon after my arrival in Cornwall, her unwilling confidant, though I did not understand much of what I was privy to till much later. I certainly did not like her or wish to be near her but was obliged to see her and talk to her alone regularly.

It all happened by chance. To eke out what must

68

have been a frugal existence—I don't know what she lived on—she had acquired the Doublebois concession on Corona. Corona was a firm that made fizzy drinks that were far and away the favourite of all of us children. If you wanted a bottle you had to go and knock on her back door. She had crates of full bottles in her cool little cellar and crates of empties ready for collection outside the back door. Corona bottles came pint-sized and were secured with an intricate wire arrangement attached to a ceramic cork which had a red rubber washer round it. You opened the bottle by holding it in your two hands and pressing on the wire on either side of the neck with your thumbs until the whole arrangement moved past some sort of fulcrum. Then the cork was released and the pressure from within blew the bottle open with a satisfying pop. If you had been shaking it, or if it was too warm, the opening pop was an explosion, followed by a foaming tide and you lost half of the contents. Our favourites were cherryade (sweetly disgusting) and ginger beer (probably would still taste good to me today).

Every Sunday dinner in summer Jack and I were allowed to have a glass each with our meal. But there was a difficulty. Miss Polmanor would not trade on a Sunday. That was against her strict Methodist religious convictions. The same widespread convictions that had ensured, to Uncle Jack's frustration, that there was no pub in Dobwalls and that most of Wales was shut on a Sunday. So we had to buy our bottle the day before during normal shopping hours. On a Saturday morning, with Jack and with last week's empty, worth a penny or ha'penny back, it was an enjoyable errand. We could choose the flavour—if there was a choice—and carry the new full treasure carefully home to be stored somewhere cool for Sunday. But the errand was sometimes forgotten on a busy Saturday and disappointment stared us in the face on Sunday morning. On one such morning Auntie Rose cannily sent me alone on what looked like a pointless mission.

Acting on instructions I said, 'Sorry, Miss Polmanor, but Uncle Jack was working on the line yesterday, war work. Auntie Rose was ill in bed and Jack and I were at choir practice. Could you let us have a bottle of pop, please?'

'I can't sell you anything on a Sunday,' she said in the shocked tones of one who was appalled at even being asked. 'Mr and Mrs Phillips know that.' She was one of the few who did not call them Auntie Rose and Uncle Jack. ' 'Tis against the Scriptures. I'm surprised at them sending you.'

Somehow I had the wit to say, 'Oh, but they didn't, Miss Polmanor. I thought it by myself. I thought you might make an exception.'

She must have liked that because I saw a rare faint smile on her face and she sounded more gentle. 'Tisn't for me to make exceptions, young man. 'Tis for God. Be you worth an exception?'

I couldn't handle the problem of thinking how God might make an exception for me, so gave up. 'Sorry to bother you, Miss Polmanor.' I turned away, looking into a Corona-less Sunday lunch.

'Just a minute, young man. Did you say that you were at choir practice?'

I was too honest by far, bearing in mind her Wesleyan faith. 'Yes, Miss Polmanor. But it was Church of England choir practice, at St Peter's,

70

not at Mr Buckroyd's.'

'That don't matter, boy. You was doing God's will as you saw it.'

Is that what I was doing, I thought to myself.

'I can't sell you anything on a Sunday. That's for sure. But, if you're very good, I could *give* you a bottle to take with you and you could pay me tomorrow.'

I can't remember what I said, if anything.

'Not a word to anyone, mind, or my life will be a misery.'

I wasn't foolish enough to respond to that with a clever remark or old enough to have even thought of one. I stood, respectfully hopeful.

'And only because you was singing to the glory of God. This is just between you, me and Him.' She gestured upwards. 'Promise?'

I did so fervently.

'And will you be good if I do?'

Another ardent assurance. She certainly demanded her pound of flesh on His behalf.

'There you are, then. And give thanks to God when you drink it.'

I took it, thanked her and God and ran for it.

Of course, the minute I was home Auntie Rose had to know how I had drawn ginger beer from that particular stone. When I told her she quietly smiled and I was made to promise to take the money straight after school. Uncle Jack's eyes lit up when he heard the story. 'A chink in God's armour,' he laughed. 'Who would've thought it.'

Unfortunately this led to a further intimacy: when I took the money she asked me in. Her house was more old-fashioned than anything I had seen, packed with bric-à-brac, mementoes, religious texts and biblical pictures. There was one item that stood centre on the sideboard that was unmissable: a silver-framed photo of a man. It was turned into a modest shrine, standing on a little tapestry with candlesticks on either side.

'He was a saint,' said Miss Polmanor, as she saw me look at him. 'He died abroad for me and Jesus and now I live for both of them. That's my vocation, willed on me by God.'

The man just looked ordinary to me, someone from another age. I don't even remember feeling curious. Realising that I was some sort of favourite, Auntie Rose usually saw that Jack was working on our vegetable patch in the garden with Uncle Jack, something Jack enjoyed and I didn't, and sent me to buy the Corona on my own. I think she did it as a kindness—to Miss Polmanor, not to me. Objections from me were overridden: it became my job. Miss Polmanor gave me texts and talks and even the occasional glass of Corona along with oblique references to the 'saint' that were lost on me but which left me uncomfortable. I got the impression that he was a missionary who had died of something or other in darkest somewhere or other. She liked to open herself, no matter how slightly, to me and even patted my head once and gave me a half-hearted hug, which enveloped me in a two-level, sweet-and-sour sickly smell that nearly caused me to run for it. But we were used to being the recipients of unwanted embraces or cuffs and were skilled at dodging them. After that I generally managed to keep the plentiful furniture between her and me. Somehow I had slipped through the net of her disapproval of all things young—and especially vacky—and had her bottled-up affection.

I used to hope for Elsie to rescue me from all this if she was in, but when Miss Polmanor answered the door to me with my sixpence and empty bottle Elsie was gone in a flash and I am sure that Miss Polmanor was glad to see her go in spite of her constant denunciations of Elsie's unwillingness ever to stay in—probably to avoid yet more futile, pious indoctrination.

Miss Polmanor rode her bicycle into Dobwalls to shop and do her good works, often, so Auntie Rose said, to the exasperation of Buckroyd. She was soon round the Wesleyan minister's neck about us vackies playing in the Methodist graveyard at dinner break. ' 'Tis sacrilege, Mr Buckroyd. Disturbin' the dead like that.'

'I don't think the dead mind too much, Miss Polmanor.'

'They make up profane words to hymn tunes. I've heard they.'

'So do our children, Miss Polmanor.'

'But not so profane as they.'

'Well, they're more—er—inventive.'

'More sinful.'

'There's a war on, Miss Polmanor.'

And, in the rumour and gossip that always rides in tandem with war—I mean our private war—stories abounded of vackies who behaved outrageously or were treated with cruelty.

'Have you ever heard? Over to Tremabe they chopped off all the chickens' heads. Every living one o' 'em. Two little savages, only seven years old.'

'No. Is that so, my dear?'

'And down to Warleggan they slaughtered lambs

73

Vacky boys in the graveyard of the Wesleyan chapel, Jack on right

in the fields, fired a rick. 'Tis bloody mayhem, I'm telling you—oh, sorry, Mrs. I didn't mean to—but 'tis terrible.'

' 'Tis like a plague: the eleventh plague of Egypt, the plague of children.'

'Oh, no, no, no. We got two. They'm nice. I like 'em. My missus dotes on 'em.'

And, after their gossip, villagers strode off down the main road along which Dobwalls was strung, tut-tutting or doubting, according to their views.

There was one story that was ubiquitous, told in every village in the county. 'You know that farmer up the edge of the Moor, Penmalligan. He had two vackies billeted on he.'

'Ar. Boy 'n' a maid.'

'Well, he locked they in the linney all night, then took his strap to 'em after breakfast. His breakfast. They din' get none. They was nine and ten years old. Well, their father got to year. In the Guards, he is. Grenadiers. Back from Dunkirk.'

'Yes, they was there, I read it.'

'Well, he went AWOL, went to Penmalligan's farm, punched he all round his own farmyard, then took his kids off with him back to Lunnon. 'Twas a proper job.'

'Have you heard of anyone else giving they vackies what for?'

'No. Everyone round yere be giving it up for Lent.'

And though such events always took place in the next village but one, the mythical guardsman was a famous and cautionary figure.

*   *   *

Uncle Jack took Jack and me in hand. 'Who started it all?'

'They called us slum kids.'

'And what did you call them?'

'Turnips.'

'What else?'

'Yokels.'

'What else?'

'Clodhoppers.'

'Hmm. Who called who names first?'

This was lost in the mists of time.

He put his arms round us confidentially. 'Listen, boys. You can't call people names when you're living in a village full of self-righteous, Godbothering hypocrites. So don't do it.'

'No, Uncle Jack. Sorry, Uncle Jack.'

'I know they're a lot of Bible-punching Tories, but try to make friends with 'em. We're fighting the Germans, not each other.'

CHAPTER SIX

Quiet but intense excitement in the Phillips household. Gwyn, their younger son, was coming home on leave. He was training somewhere. When he was called up he managed to get into the Royal Welch Fusiliers like his father. The Welch, with its archaic spelling, was a top regiment. Uncle Jack must have been pleased in that schizophrenic way he had of both hating the military and being proud of being Welsh. Tories, staff officers, authority in general, mine owners in particular, shareholders ('vested interests' was the phrase then) and

76

religion were all his targets but he was patriotic. Auntie Rose's political views were simple: she distrusted anything or anyone that put her loved ones in jeopardy. She had suffered the First World War with Uncle Jack being at the front and invalided out. She didn't need any of that again, and Gwyn was her youngest and most vulnerable. Her daughter, Rose, was relatively safe in Barry, South Wales. Older son Len, Leonard Llewellyn, was ground crew in the RAF, which seemed as good as she could hope for. Both of them were married, something which gave a feeling of danger shared, of security, no matter how false. But Gwyn was single, all hers, and anything could happen to him. He was already a corporal, another source of unspoken pride for Uncle Jack but of no comfort to Auntie Rose.

She was on the platform to meet the train; Uncle Jack was working on the line in the valley; Jack and I swung on the wire fence behind the wash-house and looked down on the station. The train blocked our view at first but as it pulled away we saw Auntie Rose in the arms of a soldier, his back to us, her head buried in his shoulder, then raised to look into his eyes; we could see hers shining from fifty yards away. He was dark, not very tall, had a kitbag and rifle. Instead of taking the usual route, walking to our end of the platform, crossing the line (illegally) and climbing the little track that many feet had worn, then ducking through the wires, they walked away from us, the long way round, down the platform to greet the porter and Mr Rawlings the stationmaster, over the bridge, up the road and down the Court. I think she wanted to show him off to anyone who was about.

We soon discovered that Gwyn was extrovert, carefree and seemed to like the world as much as we quickly grew to worship him. When I say carefree, his humour had a black, graveyard edge to it, always visible, like Uncle Jack's. He never stopped singing, a nice tenor or light baritone, I am not sure which. The reason for his musical leaning was not just the cliché of being Welsh. Uncle Jack had encouraged it, trained it since Gwyn's treble days, as a possible escape from a life of drudgery down the mines, on the railway, or in some factory. He had seen a way to help his son to escape from what had been his life. He had the right pupil, with a ready unselfconscious voice and easy invention. Every popular hymn and Welsh song was sung to us in snatches with Gwyn's (and other soldiers') subversive or filthy lyrics.

'How did you become a corporal, Gwyn?'

'I kissed the sergeant major.' He cleaned up the usual saying for us, although kissing the sergeant major face to face seemed more shocking than kissing his arse.

'Are you going to fight the Germans, Gwyn?' I asked him when his leave was drawing to a close.

'No. More training in the mountains, boy. Bloody cold. The Brecon Beacons. It's not much fun but it's better than getting killed. They're saving us Welsh. In reserve. After the Germans have wiped out all you English we'll go in and sing 'em to death.' And he let out a burst of a Welsh patriotic tune with very unofficial English lyrics.

The immensely popular song 'We'll Meet Again' was constantly on the radio, generally delivered by Vera Lynn. Gwyn loved to parody her. He would emote extravagantly, arms thrown wide, and sing, 'We'll meet again, when they've blown up Big Ben,' holding 'Ben' for ever with massive vibrato. Seven-year-old me found this the height of musical satire.

I wondered about those mountains, unknown things to me. Our train rides to our great-aunts in Brighton took us through the South Downs; but mountains? And the Brecon Beacons? What were they? And why were they cold in the summer? Uncle Jack soon had his atlas out from the one or two shelves of Serious Books that filled the bookcase in the rarely used front room. I was in it for hour after hour while I was in Cornwall when it was too wet or cold or hot or dark to go out. And often when it wasn't. There were cities with exotic names that became battlegrounds in the war; mountains, seas, oceans, plains, deserts and rivers that were being fought over; the shapes of the continents fascinated me; the outlines of the countries, each with its own individual colour; the vast amount of pink where the thin red line had passed, nearly half of the world, it seemed, was the British Empire. I swelled with pride: our empire.

Some evenings in Gwyn's week's leave Uncle Jack went for a drink in Liskeard with him and on Sunday morning after Auntie Rose had put the roast in the oven we all walked down to Halfway House—our nearest pub down the main road into the valley, halfway to Bodmin Road station (now, prissily, Bodmin Parkway), the next stop on the line—for drinks before Sunday dinner: beer for the men, shandy for Auntie Rose, pop for Jack and me, crisps for all of us. Then back with bottles in the men's jacket pockets. We learned to value our pleasures: it was three and a half miles there, three and a half miles back, mostly uphill, singing all the way, led by Gwyn.

'Gwyn's going to be a singer after the war,' Uncle Jack had told us and anyone who would listen.

'Going to be. He never stops,' Auntie Rose complained insincerely.

She was a different person with Gwyn there, like an opened flower. Uncle Jack quietly glowed instead of his usual half-scowl. The place was lit up, full of Gwyn's song and laughter. And then he was gone.

*   *   *

The woods, in summer, became our playground. They were as good as they promised when we first saw them: endless trees to climb; little streams everywhere, some of which dried up in hot weather and others that only appeared when there had been a lot of rain. Even these were often, to our surprise, full of tiny fish, minnows or sticklebacks, which you could catch in a jam-jar and take home. But they soon died so we gave that up. These streams we dammed or re-routed; we collected watercress from them and took it home for the table. I saw a kingfisher that had built its nest far from the river and was earning a living and raising a family on one of these tiny, gurgling flows.

But it was the River Fowey that was the magnet to us. It hurried along in its dappled cavern, with deep pools that swirled mysteriously, could suck you fatally down and held fish of giant size in our imaginations. It splashed over rapids that it seemed no fish could possibly negotiate. There were little sandy beaches in places with backwaters where you could examine the insects and trout fry in close proximity, making a pool which they could not escape from until you dug a channel with your hand and watched them swim away. Tree trunks lay across it, deliberately felled or just left to make bridges for the more agile. Further upstream, beyond the limits of the Doublebois House estate, the woods thinned out and the river flowed through meadows until you traced it back to open moorland where the buzzards soared and the wind always seemed to be blowing too much. But that was quite a walk, rarely undertaken.

Of course, when they visited, our parents were taken to our magic playground. Mum, hobbling along the riverside path in unsuitable shoes—actually high heels if my memory is correct—was soon stuck over the middle of the river on one of the tree trunks, sitting down, legs astride in a very undignified manner, while we ran back and forth, climbing over her to show off our skill, offering advice that she couldn't take and laughing and yelling with glee. She would appeal to Dad, 'Billie, help me, I can't . . . I'm slipping . . .' but Dad played to the gallery of his agile sons and joined in the masculine taunts. Mum laughed too in that hopeless way she used when she couldn't do anything about a situation, though I suspect she was really hating it, just making acquiescent noises and glad to be with us.

*　　　*　　　*

One of the first things we vackies did was to build a hut in the woods. Most of the forest in the Fowey Valley was naturally deciduous but there were plantations of firs, standing in military rows. We drove in some stakes between four of these trees, cut branches for mainstays, found ferns and wove the fronds into four walls and a roof. More ferns and pine needles made a dryish comfortable floor. It was dark and womb-like in there, exciting when with someone else, frightening when alone and the sounds of the forest outside became menacing. The smell of resin was everywhere; we would go home sticky with the stuff. Jack and I, Ken, Eric and Peter Plummer, and Harold and Alan Packham created this place. It was our secret, jealously guarded.

Ken and Eric from Plymouth lived in the cramped little whitewashed bungalow across the Court with their mother. Their older brother Peter soon left, I think to join the army, and there were four more brothers, grown-up, who showed up occasionally, and a father who was sometimes seen and I don't remember. They were probably all serving somewhere or another. My mother would have called them common—probably did, and they probably were. How would a family of seven brothers, brought up in one of the tougher parts of Plymouth in the Depression, be anything else? Welsh, working-class Auntie Rose found them 'a bit rough', but they were our friends across the Court: such distinctions didn't matter. Their urban attitudes resonated with us vackies from London more than the rural ones of the Doublebois children. We, like them, were the outsiders, although to us Londoners their accents were at first indistinguishable from the local children's, something both parties hotly denied.

Elsie Plummer, their cousin, ripe with imminent puberty, was certainly 'a bit rough'; even Mrs Plummer thought so. One of her regular games was executing high kicks whenever we were playing together, generally at the entrance to the army camp. She was very proud of the height she could kick, would demonstrate it whenever possible and afforded every child, and most of the soldiers on guard duty, frequent glimpses of her knickers. When the ground was dry she would also demonstrate the splits to anyone interested, lifting her skirt to show that her knees were straight and her knickers touching the ground, providing us with a more protracted view. There wasn't room in the bungalow for a girl, she and her male cousins were approaching puberty, so Elsie was billeted out. On Miss Polmanor of all people.

Elsie was into the bungalow and our house whenever possible. Auntie Rose half disapproved of her and half sympathised. Miss Polmanor regarded Elsie as her cross to bear for the duration; she made it her mission to convert Elsie to godliness. 'I'll save that maid's soul or die in the attempt.' A hopeless cause. It must have been one of the most mismatched billetings of the whole war and I wonder if some malicious officer was settling a score with Miss Polmanor. The trouble was that besides foisting Elsie on Miss Polmanor he inflicted Miss Polmanor on Elsie, though I think Elsie was the more resilient of the two.

When Elsie first met us London vackies we thought she was a local. She vehemently denied this and faced us squarely with her direct stare and burgeoning body. 'Well, you talk like they do,' we said.

'I don't. I talk ever so different. I be from Plymouth.' She pointed vaguely. ' 'Tis over to there. My dad's in the army and my mum's gone off with a sailor so they sent me yere. I don't like it yere.'

'We do,' someone ventured.

Elsie ignored this and continued on her own tack. 'I've held the hand of a dead person.'

We just stood and stared at this revelation, imaginations racing.

'Have you really?'

'Yes.'

'Whose?' challenged a disbelieving voice.

'My granny's.'

'Oh.' The unlikely scenario gained credibility.

'I was holding her hand and she died.'

'What did you do?'

'Nothing.'

After a long reflective pause someone said, 'Do you want to play with us?'

She nodded.

'Come on, then.'

We learned later from the Plummer boys that this story was often trotted out, one of several methods Elsie used to make an impression, though it was probably true. 'If she was holding my yand I'd've been glad to die,' said Peter Plummer contemptuously. 'That was our granny too,' complained his brothers, feeling upstaged by Elsie.

But their comments were too late. Elsie was in my head, indelibly. Months later she and I were playing together and went off into the woods to explore. Anxious to impress her I took her to our secret hut and swore her to secrecy. We crawled in through the low doorway; she looked round. 'Cor, 'tis lovely and dark. Smells of resin. No one would ever know we were yere.' She settled herself. 'D'you want to play doctors?'

I was mystified.

She looked at me speculatively. 'How old be you?'

'Nearly eight.'

'I'm nearly thirteen. I'll be doctor first.'

'All right.'

'You got to take all your clothes off.'

I was flabbergasted. '*All* of them?'

'Yes.'

'My pants too?'

'Then you lie down and I examine you. I say, "What seems to be the trouble, Mr Smith?"'

'The school doctor just combed my hair for nits.'

'Do you want to play or not?'

'No.' But I did, desperately.

'You shy?'

'Yes.'

'So be I. Let's undress together.'

Clever Elsie had calmed the fears of both of us. We solemnly started to remove our clothes. Before we had got far, 'You know boys and girls 're different?'

More new territory. 'I think so.' I knew so, thanks to our cousins.

'D'you know why?'

'No.' This seemed like the safest answer. 'Hazily' would have been more truthful.

' 'Tis to make babies. You put your widdler in my twinkle then I have a baby.'

85

I giggled nervously. She was insane. 'Don't be daft.'

'True.'

'It wouldn't go.'

'No, I thought that. I don't think it works till you're married, I think. Or grown-up. Tiny little babies come out the end of your widdler. All swimming.'

I let out an 'Eeargh' of disgust.

But she was relentless. 'The husband has to lie on top of the wife, then it works. All husbands and wives do it. Your mum and dad did it to get you.'

'Shut up,' I muttered sullenly, not wanting to imagine such an event.

'The baby grows for nine months in yere, then comes out.'

'Babies are too big.' I had caught her on a practical level.

But even that was no good. She just agreed. 'I know. I don't get it. The woman screams, so it mustn't half hurt. I don't think I want babies.'

We were both out of our depth. 'You made it all up.'

'The animals do it, too. You watch. I have. Nobody saw me. Crago's bull. Blige me. His widdler. You should see. They all laughed.'

I was shocked into protest. 'We're not animals,' and searched for an argument to refute her. Sunday school came to mind. 'We got souls. The vicar said we've got souls and animals haven't.'

'What does he know? Be you going to play doctor, then?'

'No. I don't like you.'

'Yes, you do.'

And she was right. I did. I, sort of, loved her.

86

She spoke with a calm authority that was thrilling and disturbing. Like every other child learning the facts of life unofficially as we did I thought of my parents doing it: no. It was all too grotesque. I went home, stared at Auntie Rose and Uncle Jack and tried to imagine them engaged in something so rude and unlikely. No, not possible. I cornered Uncle Jack in the garden where we wouldn't be overheard. 'Uncle Jack, have we got souls?'

He was always glad to hold forth on this subject. 'Nobody knows, boy, though they say they do.'

'Nobody in the whole world?'

'No. But if you ask me, it's all tripe. All of it. All religion. Rubbish.'

'So we *are* just like the animals?'

'I wouldn't say that, boy. We got *minds*.' And he grinned with satisfaction at this opportunity to make his prime, anti-religious, point. How could he know that we'd just been having our first conversation about sex?

Auntie Rose was feeding the hens.

'Auntie Rose, have we got souls?'

'Course we have, my love. What d'you think we are, animals?'

'Uncle Jack says we haven't.'

'What does he know? Heathen.'

There appeared to be nothing but confusion on the subject in the adult world, so how could Elsie know? But the assurances of her still childish but swelling body against mine, the changes in herself she pointed out so proudly, the persistent rumours of the truth that I encountered among the older children and the overwhelming evidence in the countryside all round us soon undermined my disbelief. So, when the other boys were busy

87

elsewhere, the promise of a breathless, dry session of doctors with Elsie—full of intimacy yet reserve—created a trembling inexplicable excitement that was quite fulfilled by the cool, clinical little scenes we acted out in our pine-scented surgery in the woods.

CHAPTER SEVEN

Autumn introduced me to different new pleasures in the countryside. Blackberrying with Auntie Rose on the Slates came first. The Slates was the embankment beside the stretch of railway just below Doublebois before it disappeared into the woods. This embankment sloped down into the Rabbit Field, a long narrow field which lay between the main road and the railway and eventually merged into the woodland. The Slates was made up of the local slate blasted from the side of the valley when the railway was cut into it and the ballast laid down. Nothing but brambles and thistles would grow there. On the far side of the line was the goods yard, Blamey and Morgan's mill and the animal pens. Auntie Rose, with bowls and jugs in a basket, led us out of the Court, through the crossroads and very quietly through the gate into the Rabbit Field. This was the moment for Jack and me to take off, hullooing and yelling down the slope. It was only then, among the thistles and hummocks of this not very fertile field, that you realised how aptly it was named: it became alive with rabbits scattering in every direction before they disappeared.

Next, the Slates: steeply sloped, dark-grey Cornish slates sliding under your feet. Don't fall over, they cut; and brambles scratch. Bushes in clumps all round you, big fat blackberries. Pick four or five, eat one, pick some more, eat some more, fingers and lips stained purple. Stop and stare while a train which has stopped at Doublebois gathers speed just above your head, huge and threatening from where you stand below its wheels. Sometimes an express would roar by just above you, thrilling in its power and noise, belching smoke if it was labouring up the gradient on its way to Plymouth, or rattling happily, only a thin plume of steam, as it virtually freewheeled going west, down the valley. And waving, always waving at the drivers, firemen, passengers, guard. Then back to the business in hand, literally, until Auntie Rose said, 'All right. These yere'll do. We'll come back next week, there'll be a new crop ripe by then.' She always picked more than Jack's and my scrambling, purple-stained efforts put together.

Auntie Rose turned those blackberries into jam for the winter, all the jam she could make on our meagre sugar ration, and blackberry-and-apple pies for Sunday dinner, with custard usually, or rarely, and if we were very lucky, with clotted cream: the best pudding in the world, hot or cold.

The other riveting activity of autumn was the harvest. As the binders went round and round the fields, leaving a diminshing stand of oats or barley in the middle—no wheat was planted in wet, windblown Cornwall—we would stand the cut sheaves into regularly spaced little stooks and keep an eye out for rabbits. Generally two children would work with a man, the children gathering the sheaves, the man expertly stooking them so that they wouldn't fall over in any wind or rain that might come before we gathered them onto carts and built ricks ready for the threshing, the next excitement to come. Everyone turned out for the harvest, a country tradition. We children, promised payment for our time, set to with a will as we eagerly worked out how much we had earned at so much an hour. We would turn up at the farmer's door a few days later for our money and find out it was always less than we thought we had been promised, probably another country tradition.

But the real fun for most of us was the rabbits. As the tractor cut more and more corn the rabbits would retreat into the centre of the field, still invisible, frightened inwards by the noise. In fact they stood a better chance if they broke early with only a few yards to the safety of their burrows in the hedges. I always thought of the early ones, who shot out and were gone before we could move, as the clever ones, whereas they were probably the most frightened. As the climax drew near the rabbits would break with increasing frequency, but now they had a long run, had to thread their way through many clutching hands, past stabbing pitchforks and—generally their doom—the dogs. The dogs weren't allowed into the corn after them, no matter how excited by the scents. So, as each rabbit broke, there was a mad hallooing and barking, generally ending in a growl, a sudden death and a warm furry body swiftly disappearing into a capacious pocket, to be gutted, skinned and into the pot. Some got away, and the dogs would scrabble fruitlessly about in the hedges, barking frenziedly: if they didn't get them in the open, they were unlikely to succeed in the rabbits' natural havens.

Uncle Jack was a master at rabbit-catching. Into the field straight after his day on the track, he would arrive as cutting was nearly finished. That tiny, round figure could cover a few yards in a flash. Jack and I were always racing him down the Court and never won. A rabbit would break, a dive, a quick twist with his hands, and he would wink at us as the little bundle went into the pocket inside his jacket. When he had got two or three he would whistle to us and off we went home for tea to discover he generally had another one he had caught when we weren't looking. I find it almost unbelievable now that round little Uncle Jack could snatch at and catch a passing rabbit, quicker even than the dogs. But he could; I saw it. And he was not unique.

We were always on at him to let us kill one, and I can remember experimenting with tentative, inadequate rabbit punches as I held up some poor creature by its hind legs and chopped tentatively away at the back of its neck with the side of my hand until Uncle Jack took it from me and ended its pain and fear. At first I was the squeamish young townie, half afraid of anything living and wild, and not really wanting to hurt it. Quite soon that was buried under my wish to demonstrate my—what? Manliness? Competence? I don't know, but thus are many sorts of killers made, out of wishing to belong. We caught rabbits all the time in the gins and snares that were in constant use all round us, and, as the rabbits were often still alive when we came to inspect the traps, we had plenty of opportunities to improve our techniques.

I became adept, preferring to hold the neck in one hand and hind legs in the other. Then a stretch and sharp twist. Apart from the centuries-old farmer/rabbit war, they were a very welcome addition to our wartime meat ration, but that was just an excuse for my willingness to kill.

When threshing time came a tractor would tow the threshing machine round the local farms: a clanking, smelly thing that produced clouds of chaff to make you sneeze, driven by a belt fitted on to a tractor. We would gather at each farm to join in. Then it was the turn of rats and mice to be the quarry. There were always some who had made the newly built ricks their home and larder in just a few days. But as the sheaves were dismantled and forked into the thresher it was slaughter. The bigger boys loved to spear them with pitchforks as they appeared and the dogs made short work of those that were missed. There was always the thrill of daring to corner a rat when legend had it that they would fight to the death, leap for your throat or somehow bite you. But I never saw any person or dog remotely threatened by these terrified creatures.

And then, as the leaves started to fall, I can clearly remember standing at the crossroads in Doublebois looking out over the valley and watching flocks of birds heading relentlessly south; I don't know what they were but they were big and small birds and big and small groups and in vast numbers. The biggest and most spectacular flocks, though, were the starlings just finding their roost for the night. They wheeled and dived and rose and spread, bunching up and thinning out from dense black clouds into long wisps before sinking down into the woods and disappearing. I have never liked starlings in the garden, always in numbers, coming noisily down in their glossy blue-black plumage, strutting about and bullying the other birds, the storm troopers of the back lawn; but their aerobatics en masse were unforgettable. I was never up early enough to see them rise the following morning.

The climax of autumn was the harvest festival when the church was full of donated fruit, vegetables—principally marrows which people were glad to get rid of—and sheaves of corn, and we all belted out 'We Plough The Fields And Scatter', and 'Come Ye Thankful People, Come'. After this celebration the fields were bare, the grass stopped growing in the pastures, tractors criss-crossed the cornfields, ploughing-in the stubble, followed by squabbling crowds of seagulls, crows, lapwings and the inevitable starlings. And the world turned brown.

*   *   *

A few months later the furious winter of 1940-1 took hold. The village pumps were encased in ice and the wind whipped the snow down off Bodmin Moor making six-foot drifts in the middle of Dobwalls. Snow was a rarity in the south-westerly airstreams of Cornwall. For the Doublebois children the mile and a half walk to school became an ordeal involving red ears and noses, chilblains, chapped fingers, soaked woollen gloves with icicles on them, wet feet and necks from the melted snow that spilled into every gap in our clothing, especially over and into our hobnail boots. We had

93

cold feet all day. Not one of us had wellies as I recall; there was no rubber to spare to make such things for children.

When we walked home was the time for games: slides in the village street which annoyed the grown-ups, snowballs thrown at each other as we walked, ran and trudged the mile and a half back. We waded into snowdrift after snowdrift until we were frozen, soaking and bored with it. Then, oh then, the warm range in the kitchen of the Phillips' cottage, fingers and faces going red in the heat, hot drinks, cosiness and Auntie Rose presiding over it all.

Going to bed was the next ordeal. Undress downstairs into warmed pyjamas, no heat up there, but a lovely stone hot-water bottle in the bed to put your feet on as shivering you scrambled in to snuggle down into a billowy mattress, pillows, blankets and eiderdown. In the morning the windows were an etched miracle of frost patterns, often with the ice on the inside, condensation from our night-time breathing, which you could pick at or draw on with your fingernail before reluctantly getting out and diving into clothes that Auntie Rose had left warming by the range all night.

The children arranged a mass snowball fight one dinner break; vackies versus village kids. It included every child in the district between the ages of five and fifteen and got utterly out of hand—not that it was ever in it. Waves of schoolchildren surged up and down the road between the village school and the Methodist chapel hurling ice and snow or just shouting. When the bells sounded, while some law-abiding souls went in to school, the rest of us spilled over

94

into fields and chased each other to Duloe Bridge. The climax was a snowball shoot-out as the wan winter daylight faded. We swaggered back into class in front of the admiring looks of the more timid kids to have the smirks wiped off our faces by Mrs Langdon, our Junior Vackies mistress, normally the kindest of women, and Miss Shepherd of the village school, a tiny, bird-like creature, who laid their rulers mercilessly across our chapped and tingling fingers.

And once, when Mr Evans, the elderly village-school headmaster, was absent, tiny Miss Shepherd was forced to bring out their school cane and wield it on several of the bigger boys—vackies and village kids—for a group transgression: chanting blasphemous versions of *Hymns Ancient and Modern* in public. Miss Shepherd was halfway down the row of proffered backsides when the cane, groaning under its excessive burden, gave up the ghost and snapped in two. Miss Shepherd burst into tears and the row of unyielding bottoms returned to their seats.

*   *   *

A weekly ordeal was the letter home. Auntie Rose was adamant. We were never allowed to miss. I regarded it as a chore to be endured; it must have been torture for Jack. One winter evening I sat at the table chewing a pencil while Auntie Rose mended socks with a letter from Gwyn on her lap. She was upset and not inclined to be indulgent to my whinges.

'I can't think of anything to write.'
'You say that every week.'

*Auntie Rose, Jack and me by
the never-used front door*

I was as foolish as ever. Walking in where I should never go. 'You've read that letter from Gwyn hundreds of times.'

'And I shall probably read it hundreds more.' I froze at the tone in her voice. 'They said he was only going training back home in Wales. Now they've sent him abroad. Abroad. Where? Haven't they ever heard of embarkation leave?' Her voice had risen to a querulous high and she stared at me as though it were my fault and I had the answer.

Intimidated, I offered, 'Uncle Jack said they didn't give them leave because they didn't want to warn the German submarines. Careless talk costs lives.' This was a wartime slogan which I piously trotted out.

'What does he know about it?' she growled.

'That means the army were protecting our soldiers,' I tried.

'The army? Protecting our soldiers?' She raised her head from her mending. Her eyes were hollow black bottomless holes as she looked at me. Her voice slashed across the room. 'When did that ever enter their heads?' I stared at this apparition, a moment ago sober, comforting Auntie Rose, now someone looking out of hell. I think she must have seen my dismay because her eyes and voice returned to normal. To my relief she went on. ' "Address, care of the War Office". Care of . Huh.' She changed again, lost in her own world; I wasn't there. 'Like they took care of the boys from Jack's pit in the last lot.'

I was too curious to keep silent. 'What's the last lot, Auntie Rose?'

She was still lost. 'The last war. Jack was the only one who came back alive to our village in

97

Wales. The only one. It's why we left: every woman staring at me as if it was my fault.' She shuddered and returned to the present, waving Gwyn's letter accusingly at me again. 'Ink on paper instead of a person here in your life. That's all there is: letters. And every letter from Gwyn is one page long. That's all he can manage. One page.'

'Two sides,' I tried helpfully.

'It's not enough. You write two pages home to your mam and dad this week. Two. D'you hear?'

This awful sentence took my breath away. 'That's *four* sides.'

'I know how many it is.'

'I've never written four sides.'

'You can this week.'

The awful injustice of this made me reckless. 'That's not fair. We shouldn't have to write at all. It was her sent us away.' As soon as I had said it I wished I hadn't. I tried not to catch her eye and muttered, 'Well, she did.'

'What?' she said quietly.

'I didn't mean it.'

'Don't you ever say anything like that again about your mother. Or your father.'

'I was only moaning about writing letters.'

'Never. D'you hear?'

'Yes, Auntie Rose. Sorry, Auntie Rose,' I muttered miserably. 'I didn't mean it.'

'I don't care what you meant. Never.' It was the first time I ever saw her really angry with me, even though she must have known it was only childishness on my part. 'I have to stop myself writing *fifty* sides to Gwyn, and I can hardly spell my name. You're supposed to be clever.'

I was trying not to cry. 'Just because you're

upset about Gwyn I've got to write four sides, a whole blinking book. It's not fair.'

'I know it's not fair, boy. Nothing is. Listen. Who did your shoelaces up for you before you could do your own?'

'Mum, I suppose. And Dad sometimes.'

'Your mam and dad. Exactly. And do you think they minded?'

'Dunno.'

'No, my Terry, they didn't mind. You can be sure of that. Because they love you. And your brother. They love you both . . . and your shoelaces . . . and your first teeth when you lost 'em . . . and the locks they cut from your hair. I've still got some of Len's and Rose's and Gwyn's. Even the clippings when they cut your toenails.'

'Ergh.'

'Yes. Everything about you. So. You write them four sides about your shoelaces, is it?'

'Nobody can write four sides about shoelaces.'

'I would jump for joy if I got four sides from Gwyn.'

'If they were about shoelaces you'd think he'd gone barmy.'

So, Gwyn was abroad, in North Africa, the only place the war was really going on at that moment, except over London. Perhaps his embarkation leave had been when we met him and he had kept quiet about it. We looked at pictures in the papers and during our rare visits to the cinema at the newsreels, which showed Italian soldiers surrendering in their tens of thousands, long columns of them walking across the desert guarded by the occasional casual Tommy with a rifle slung over his shoulder. We searched to see if

99

it was Gwyn, our hero. We seemed to be winning. It was all an illusion: the Germans led by Rommel hadn't even arrived there yet.

CHAPTER EIGHT

Jack and I used to go shopping with Auntie Rose once a week in Liskeard, four miles away, the next stop on the train. There, with pocket money supplemented by our parents, we bought our weekly treats: for Jack it was generally an Army cap badge, for me a Dinky Toy.

Jack's cap badges, mounted on a green baize cloth, were quite something. He must have got most of the regiments of the British Army, a magnificent collection, which, as it grew, he would unfurl and we would gloat over: the Sphinx of the Gloucesters, for their service in Egypt, the little badge worn on the back of their caps because they fought a heroic rearguard action; the many variations of the cross of St Andrew of Scottish regiments, some with exotic names: the Argyll and Sutherland Highlanders, the Black Watch (whatever was that?). We loved the rearing white horse of our own Royal West Kents; romantic names like the Green Howards from Yorkshire; the hunting horn of the Duke of Cornwall's Light Infantry, now our local regiment. The skull and crossbones of the 17th/21st Lancers with 'Death or Glory' scrolled under them easily imprinted themselves into the imaginations of romantically bloodthirsty boys; Uncle Jack's Royal Welch Fusiliers with its curious misspelling and motto of

'*Ich dien*' ('I serve' in German, though we didn't know that); I could go on. I think he had over a hundred and I learned the geography of the country from those badges and much of our military history, all seen in a heroic glow. We were in the middle of a war for our survival and these were our saviours.

My Dinky Toys were just as important: we had sea battles with *HMS Hood*, *Valiant*, *The Prince Of Wales*—all sent to the bottom in the real war with terrible loss of life even as we played our games. I went doggedly on playing with *Hood* long after the real one was gone in such a dramatic sudden fashion, hoping that somehow she would rise from the bottom. We had aerial dogfights, Spitfires and Hurricanes shot Messerschmitts, Heinkels and Dorniers out of the sky. We raided Germany with Wellingtons, Blenheims and Halifaxes. With Sunderland flying boats we saved our convoys from U-boats. Panzer tanks were blown apart by Churchills. Foot soldiers, lying down firing, running, were placed behind table legs, some in historic costume, but all involved in this war. There were Bren Carriers, machine guns and some artillery which actually fired. Even German soldiers were there, to be knocked over and killed again and again as they lost battle after battle in the front room out of Auntie Rose's way, or in the hall, where they were laid out for us to admire without anyone ever likely to tread on them. Jack sold his wonderful collection years later, after he was married, to help pay for the conversion of the very nice coach house he and his wife had bought. But even then, when I was well into my twenties, it seemed like an act of vandalism to me. My Dinky

Toys disappeared over the years in a much less useful fashion: I lost them or grew out of them and swapped them for other things now long forgotten.

The trips to Liskeard were regular weekly outings. But the great events that filled us with excitement were the much rarer twenty-two-mile train rides to Plymouth. On to the 9.40 a.m. stopping train, over Moorswater Viaduct and some spectacular views, especially down on to the Looe branch line that went right beneath us like a model; out of Liskeard station on another viaduct over another part of the same branch line. We, on the main line, would rattle on to Menheniot and St Germans. At last, Saltash, looking over the Torpoint ferry, and the Royal Albert Bridge, known to us all as Saltash Bridge. 'Built by Isambard Kingdom Brunel', it announced at either end. What a name. It was the crossing point back into England.

There followed the slow rumble over the bridge, guarded by a sentry at either end. Local legend said that it moved a foot every time a train crossed. I multiplied the number of trains each week by the number of weeks since the bridge was built in 1859, then wondered why it hadn't either edged itself up the Tamar or sidled miles out to sea.

The sight of the warships, low, grey and stark, indescribably menacing, lying in the Tamar Estuary, and Devonport Docks; then Plymouth and the Hoe; the statue of Drake with his bowls, a stylish reminder of how to reduce the enemy to size; pasties that tasted of potato and pepper but had never seen meat. Jack and I saved pocket money for these trips for yet more Dinky Toys and Army cap badges, ones too rare to be found in rural Liskeard.

Over these expeditions presided Auntie Rose with two shopping bags that became loaded and we all struggled with as she led us first from queue to queue then, when the serious business was done, from shop window to shop window. A cameo brooch was pinned to her best blouse and a silver-and-blue enamel butterfly brooch to her lapel. She wore a shapeless hat that required hatpins to hold it crammed onto her long, thick brown hair, done up in a bun.

We were waiting one evening in Plymouth North Road station buffet for a train that was very late. 'Bombing up the line' was the dark rumour. Jack had bought a miniature sheath knife in its leather sheath, something he had been coveting and saving for for ages. He kept taking it from the shopping bag, unclipping the press-stud fastening round the handle and half withdrawing the glistening blade. Our heads bent over it as we experimented: should he hang it from his belt at the side or secretly at the back like a hunter's knife? It was a formidable purchase. The date was 20 March 1941. It was a Thursday, the first of the two nights on which the Luftwaffe wiped the centre of Plymouth from the face of the earth.

'Come on, boys,' said Auntie Rose. 'Put that knife away till the proper time. When you get home you play with that, not in yere. You'll lose it.'

She was interrupted by the sound of a distant siren. The whole buffet went silent. 'Oh *Duw*, what was that?' she breathed.

'An air-raid siren,' said Jack superfluously.

'They're a long way—'

She drew in her breath as the heart-stopping,

low-pitched whirr and whine that develops into the shattering wail of a siren started up close by. The voices broke out again into a hubbub and a Devon accent rose above them all to say, 'All passengers in the subway, please. At once. Come along now, my lovelies. Let's be 'avin' you.'

We all hurried out on to the platform and headed down the ramps into the subways under the tracks. The sound of gunfire was clearly audible some way off. Auntie Rose gathered us on either side of her on a bench, shopping bags on the floor before us.

'Are they bombs?' I asked Jack.

'No, they're our guns, shooting the Jerries down. Bombs whistle.' He was rooting about in the shopping bags. Suddenly there was panic in his voice. 'My knife. Where's my knife? My new sheath knife is gone.'

Auntie Rose grabbed a bag. 'Perhaps it's in this one. Yere, let's see.'

But Jack was gone, racing down the subway out of sight. 'I left it in the buffet. I left it in the buffet.'

Auntie Rose was distraught. 'Come back, come back, boy, you can't . . .' Her voice faded into disbelief. 'He's gone.'

I had been searching in the first bag. 'Here's the knife, Auntie Rose. It's in this bag. I've got it here. Jack, I got it. Come back. Come back.' And I set off after Jack, ignoring Auntie Rose's agonised voice as the tumult outside grew louder. I flew between the huddled groups of people, turned a corner and stared up the slope towards platform-level. No Jack; he had already gone. As I started to run up the slope there was an even louder bang than before and bits of glass and debris flew about at platform-level. I stopped, terrified, and stood bawling near the bottom of the slope, afraid to move, when hands grabbed me and pulled me back round the corner.

' 'Ere, boy, come yere. I got you. You can't stand out there.'

I sobbed, 'Let me go. My brother. My brother's up there.'

'What? Your brother?'

'He lost his knife. We've got it.'

'What you talking about?'

Before I could say more I heard Auntie Rose's voice. 'Here, Terry. Here he is. With me. He came back.'

And there stood Jack. His courage, like mine, had failed at the sight and sound of the real war. Auntie Rose led us back to our bench, sat down and enfolded us both. 'Oh boys, come yere. You give me heart failure, you did. Both of you.'

God knows what hell we had put her through in those few moments. How do you explain to their parents that your two charges ran up into the bombing and were blown to bits looking for a sheath knife that was in your shopping bag all the time?

'I was going to go,' Jack assured me. 'It was only that you stopped me.'

'So was I,' I affirmed, equally inaccurately.

We spent the night sitting on the bench while the inferno raged above us. My principal memory, after the initial knife panic, was that, no matter how I shook with fright, the bench, which sat about ten people, always quaked at a different rhythm, and I couldn't get my bottom synchronised to the common tempo of terror.

The next morning was the first day of spring. We stood among glass and bits on the platform till a train took us across the miraculously unscathed Saltash Bridge. Plymouth was ablaze, smoke hung everywhere; a high proportion of the bombs had been incendiary. The warships still lurked, apparently intact, in Devonport Docks and the Tamar Estuary, out of the way. Or perhaps their fire had been so intense that it was easier for the bombers to unload onto the undefended civilian centre of the city. Apparently the RAF had ready four antiquated Gloster Gladiator biplanes as air defence. I am not sure whether they ever actually took off.

At each station groups of people met the train to ask for news or just to stare at us. And there at the end of the platform at Doublebois stood Uncle Jack looking ridiculously small and vulnerable till he saw the three of us waving wildly from a window. Then his shut face burst open into a grin that threatened to tear it in two. He hurried down the platform, took her shopping bags from her, put them on the ground and hugged Auntie Rose. It was a rare enough event to see them touching, let alone this display. He just said, 'Oh *Duw*, girl. There you are. There you are.'

'Of course I am. What d'you think? Let me go, you fool. People are watching.' She was flushed and pleased.

'You looked after her, boys, did you, for me?'

We couldn't wait to tell him about it. 'It was triffic, Uncle Jack.'

'I was ever so scared.'

'I'll bet you were, boy. I thought I'd got rid of you all at last. But there's no peace for the wicked,

106

is there?'

*   *   *

All of that day in the sky to the east hung a pall of smoke which turned to a red glow at dusk. Then the bombers returned.

A small crowd of us gathered in the gardens of the cottages to watch, a safer place than the subway under North Road station. In the distance there were flashes and distant crumps while the searchlights reflected off the smoke pall. The glow under it which was Plymouth grew brighter.

'Oh, God, 'tis not possible.'

'Will anyone be left?'

Miss Polmanor had the explanation for it all. ' 'Tis hell here on earth. 'Tis the inferno come to punish us.'

'Not us.' Someone pointed at the pyre in the distance. 'Them.'

'Let us pray to God to strike Hitler dead.'

'If God wanted Hitler dead he wouldn't wait for *her* to ask,' muttered another.

The Plummers, joined by Elsie, stood silently and watched their city being destroyed. Elsie didn't know if her mother, who had run off with the sailor while her father was away in the Army, was there or not.

'Are you sure my mum's not there, Auntie Rose?'

'Course not, my lovely. Don't you worry.' Auntie Rose sounded convincing.

A neighbour added quietly, ' 'Er's crying for her mother; 'er mother never gave 'er a moment's thought.'

'Is that what's happening in London to our mum and dad?' asked Jack.

Uncle Jack was stumped for a moment. 'No, it's not nearly so—London's enormous, Plymouth's small—it just looks—worse . . .' he trailed off feebly.

'It's why we'm all vackies,' said a Plummer boy.

And Auntie Rose held me tighter than before.

The fires could not be put out; they were beyond the scope of the fire services of several cities to deal with. Most of East Cornwall and South Devon watched Plymouth burn for nearly a week, under that pall of smoke all day and that red glow at night, like a false dawn.

The Germans returned for three successive nights a month later and the whole business was repeated. This time, with shopping trips cancelled, we watched the destruction from the safety of our bedroom window, magnifying our own former heroic parts in it. Auntie Rose told us that she had spent that entire night when we were under the bombers worrying about how, if we were killed, Uncle Jack could possibly explain to our parents why she had taken us into danger in Plymouth.

CHAPTER NINE

Uncle Jack didn't take long to get Jack and me singing. His success with Gwyn, and his natural inclinations, led him. I am not so sure about Jack's enthusiasm for it but he went with it, anyway. On the other hand I was a very willing pupil and soon heard his views on many subjects as a result. One day he was taking me through a hymn, trying to get me to make sense of it. I sang without thought, breathing automatically at the end of each line:

> Time, like an ever-rolling stream,
> Bears all its sons away.
> They fly forgotten, as a dream
> Dies at the opening day.

Having listened he said casually, 'That's right, boy. Not bad. If we got to bother God this Sunday let's bother him with a decent bit of sense, eh? Not all that slop about living eternally in heaven with Him, eh? There's nothing cosy about time bearing its sons away. Pretty agnostic, really, innit, for a hymn?'

'What's agnostic, Uncle Jack?'

'It's halfway to good sense, boy. Atheism says there's no God; agnostic says I'm not sure. I don't suppose the chap that wrote any hymn's a real atheist, so we'll have to do with halfway house. Now, let's have it again but we'll hit 'em with a bit o' clever phrasing this time, so they listen. Look yere, take your breaths where I marked the page. See? Then they'll have to think a minute. Not that any of 'em do in church, but you never know.'

'There is only one God, isn't there, Uncle Jack?'

'At most.'

'Then why are church and chapel different?'

I had got him on to one of his favourite rants. He leaned in confidentially. 'Well, you see, boy, church is a lot of lying, hypocritical, God-bothering, sinful Tories.' He paused, hoping I would ask the question. I did.

'And what's chapel?'

'Chapel is church without the poetry.' Having got that one off his chest he returned with vigour to the matter in hand. 'Come on now, with sense this time. Breathe where I marked it and start off with a big 'un.'

I gave it to him as instructed, one breath for the first two lines. I could just make it. ' "Time, like an ever-rolling stream, Bears all its sons away." ' Big breath. ' "They fly forgotten," ' a quick breath, the remainder smoothly rolled out in one, 'as a dream Dies at the opening day." ' I let the last word hang and fade as my breath ran out.

There was a moment before he spoke. 'There is lovely, my Terry. There is a beautiful voice you do have there. Makes me cry to year you. A scruffy little cockney with a voice like an angel.'

But I was learning his language. 'You don't believe in angels.'

He grinned and made to cuff me. 'Only when I hear them sing.'

I dared to be too intrusive in this cosy atmosphere. 'Why don't you believe in God, Uncle Jack?'

He leaned back and looked thoughtfully at me. 'Perhaps I should turn that question round and ask you why you *do* believe.'

Like so many of his remarks this was too fundamental for an eight-year-old. I thought and stared at him, my head in a whirl. 'Everybody does.'

'Do they? I'm not so sure about your dad and mam.'

More things to grapple with that I hadn't thought about.

110

'You know, boy, I was a Christian once. Brought up into it like all of us. Then, when I was in the trenches in the last war—the one before this one, two before the next—we went forward through no-man's-land one night and captured some German dugouts. They'd made them quite homely. Very tidy, except for the dead body on one of the bunks. D'you know what was written on the wall?'

Of course I didn't as I tried to visualise this macabre domestic scene.

'Three words. In German. *Gott mit uns.* D'you know what that means?'

I was no more prescient than a moment ago.

'It means "God's on our side."' He smiled at me. 'Well. And all the time I had thought he was on ours. There was silly of me. He was backing both sides. Or neither.'

Suddenly I was on firmer ground. I came in hotly, 'Those Germans were wrong. He was on our side. We won that war.'

Uncle Jack was unperturbed, continuing to smile sadly at me. 'You're right. So we did. I forgot for a moment.'

'And we'll win this one too.' I restrained myself from pointing an imaginary Bren gun at him and making the appropriate firing noises.

'I'm sure you're right, boy. Let's hope so.'

'Can I go out to play now? The soldiers are coming back from manoeuvres.'

'Have you written to your mam and dad this week?'

'I was going to.'

'Mam and dad first.' He winked at being able to get both the last word and the last joke in. 'You don't want them thinking we're all heathens down

111

yere in Cornwall, do you?'

*   *   *

On the mantelpiece over the range in the living room of 7 Railway Cottages sat the two little brass shells in their cases with their soldered-on badges of the Prince of Wales: the three feathers and *Ich dien* on a scroll beneath, part of the cap badge of the Royal Welch Fusiliers. These shells, standing some seven or eight inches high, were treasures to us. We were fascinated by them. I think they were live. I can remember handling them again and again, feeling their weight, their shape, their menace. They were from the First World War, we knew, something to do with Uncle Jack's past. He would not tell us. At some point we had made some sort of deal with him about practising and the shells. One evening we sang 'The Ash Grove' in harmony for him and Auntie Rose. She was, as always, full of praise.

'That's lovely, boys,' she said, glowing.

Uncle Jack was more cautious. 'That's right, both of you. Not bad. You sound as though you're thinking what you're singing as well as making a beautiful sound.'

Jack was in at once. 'You going to tell us now, then, Uncle Jack?'

He looked shifty. 'Oh, well, I'm not sure.'

'You promised when we got "The Ash Grove" right,' I chimed.

Auntie Rose was instantly alert. 'Promised what?'

Uncle Jack squirmed more. 'I didn't say it was right. I said it's not bad.'

112

'He said he'd tell us the story of the Army badges on the two shells on the mantelpiece. And *Ich dien*,' we clamoured.

She looked upset. 'Oh Jack, what do they want to year all that old history for? Horrible war stories. Isn't this one enough? Our Gwyn's out there, you know.'

Uncle Jack was surprisingly mild. 'They're boys, Rose, not wurzels.'

Jack and I were already dancing round the room, firing guns and making boyish noises. 'Rat-at-tat-tat. Boom. Crash. Gwyn's a Desert Rat.'

Auntie Rose got to her feet. 'To the chickens, me. Get the eggs. The hens do talk more sense than you.'

And we were left to hear the stories of the First World War, Uncle Jack's war. 'I was in the bantams' battalion, see. If you was under five foot you weren't accepted at first. Good enough to dig coal, too small to fight, they said. Then after our High Command had let the Germans slaughter most of the good men they needed more cannon fodder so they took us titches. We made a whole battalion: the Welsh Bantams. We was in the line up against the Prussian Guards, big fine fellers, all of 'em over six foot tall. How 'bout that?'

We were horrified: he knew how to tell a story.

'Cor, that's not fair.'

'That's terrible.'

He smiled, having caught us, an easy thing to do. 'Oh, no. Not so silly. Every man's the same height when a bullet hits him. He's horizontal.'

'That's brilliant.' His views of generals and others in charge were already well known to us. 'Our High Command weren't so stupid, Uncle

Jack. They thought of that.'

He changed at once, growling angrily. 'Don't let me catch you saying any good of our leaders, boy. Especially that particular lot. They were just men like you will be sooner than you think. What were we doing fighting at all? Ernie Bevin tried to stop it with a general strike but they called him a traitor. Now, in this lot, he's in the Govern—'

Politics had got him again and he needed to be rechannelled. 'But the shells and the badges. What happened in the Great War?'

His response was sharp. 'Great War, eh? Who taught you that?'

'It's on the war memorial in the village.'

'Huh. Great.' He went into himself for a moment. 'Great, indeed.' He remembered us and gathered himself again for the story. 'First we was up against the Saxons. They was all right. They didn't like the war no more 'n we did. We used to put up a tin helmet on the end of a rifle for their snipers to take potshots at. Then they did the same for us and we scored points. The officers stopped that. Said it was giving them practice. Practice? Huh. Nobody needed it.'

'But what does "*Ich dien*" mean?'

'It's Welsh for "I serve". The Prince of Wales's feather and his motto. It's funny, "*ich*" is like German. It's more German than English. But we're Celts, dark and small, different from you Anglo-Saxons, fair-haired like them buggers.'

'Are Jack and me Saxons?'

'Were the Prussian Guards fair, too?'

'Some of 'em, yes. A thousand of them were in this wood near the Somme. There was a thousand of us, too. Our artillery started shelling them.

114

Uncle Jack sitting on a wall,
feet not reaching the ground

Their artillery started shelling us. Everyone got blown to bits. Who killed who? I don't know. Bloody fools. Trees like used matchsticks stuck in the mud. Then it got cold. German and Welsh dead frozen together, bayonets in each other. Next morning the frost had made them all white; it didn't look real, like some hellish wedding cake. "Those whom death hath joined together let no man put asunder." Seventeen of us came out alive. We got one of those insignia each.'

'But you've got two.'

'One is my mate's, Ifor Davies. Faceman from Ystrad, even smaller 'n me.'

'But if Ifor Davies was one of the seventeen why didn't he keep his badge?'

'There were plenty more battles, boy.'

It took a moment to realise the meaning that his chilling answer led us to.

'You were lucky, weren't you, Uncle Jack?' Jack said.

He looked thoughtfully at us, his mind far away. 'That's right. Lucky. Survival is an accident, boy. Chance. We learned that in the trenches but it applies to everything. It's not destiny; it's not bravery, nor cowardice; it's not God paying you back because you're good or bad; it's not even survival of the fittest. It's an accident.'

'But you lived through it. I bet you were clever and kept your head down,' I said, clinging to some certainty or other in this bleak assessment of the world by our diminutive soldier philosopher.

Uncle Jack allowed no get-outs. His voice rose with a bitter nasal tang. 'No one was clever, boy. The clever ones weren't there at all. No matter what happens to you in your life, just remember this: there's no justice. There never was and there never will be. But you've got to pretend there is. We call that being civilised.' He looked at our dismayed faces and perhaps relented a little. Anyway, he could never resist a final twist to anything he said, and though his expression remained serious, he paused, betraying his lighter intent. 'Just remember two things: it's not fair . . . and don't be late. Live your life like that and that's all you can do.'

*   *   *

I turned the massacre in the woods over and over in my mind. I acted out the scene in our woods below Doublebois, creeping through the undergrowth down by the river. I hid behind trunks as shells ripped through the foliage, tearing the boughs off; splintering the green wood, uprooting forest giants, converting trees and men to blackened stumps. Why did the thousand of our men go in here? And why did the Germans? Who wanted to capture a wood anyway? All those little Welshmen hugging the ground, getting blown to pieces in spite of their lack of inches. The event had horror, fascination and mystery, which I could leave only briefly behind as I emerged into the Rabbit Field, one of seventeen survivors going home to tea and the polished mementoes on the mantelpiece.

Uncle Jack, when pressed by us, had other stories. 'It was raining. Raining. Raining. The soaking summer of 1916. Everything was sodden. Your boots rotted on your feet. Mud, there was mud everywhere; chest-deep sometimes. Men

117

disappeared in it.'

I held my breath. 'What do you mean? Disappeared?'

'Vanished. Got swallowed up.'

'But . . . but . . . couldn't you . . .? They can't just . . . *go*.'

'Oh, couldn't they? You had to make sure you didn't follow them. Stay on the boards.'

This acceptance of death in so casual a way was harder for me to swallow than bangs and bullets.

He continued. 'But there was no clean water to drink, of course. I had to draw ours from a shell hole near by. Then it stopped raining. The water went down and we saw there'd been a dead Frog in there all the time. Just as well I boiled it.'

I was puzzled. 'What's so terrible about a dead frog?'

Jack knew. 'Stupid. He doesn't mean a frog. A Frog is a Frenchman. A French soldier.'

I was horrified. 'Uragh. Ergh.'

Jack wasn't. 'Was he all bloated like that cow in the river?'

Uncle Jack laughed. 'I'll say.'

'Oogh. I feel sick.'

Jack was enjoying himself. 'I bet he was rotting, like your boots.'

'Ergh.'

'There's lots of ways to die,' Uncle Jack reflected, looking back into his war. 'The only ones who don't die are the generals . . . except of old age.'

Auntie Rose came in. 'Now stop that, Jack. Filling the boys' heads with all that rubbish. That war's over twenty years ago.'

Uncle Jack was not abashed. 'This one's on

118

now, isn't it? D'you think it's any different? If it goes on long enough Jack could be in the army easy. Home by Christmas, we was told. How long is it since we've seen Gwyn? Over a year he's been out there.'

Our war took on a new, dreadful fascination for me. It was no longer an imaginary 'Bang-bang, you're dead,' with sanitary corpses—mostly German—and bandaged, tidy wounds. It became headless and bloated, covered in mud, mutilated and disembowelled, like the rabbits we snared then messily gutted with our penknives.

*   *   *

One morning I stood in the Court unable to believe my eyes. I stared up the railway line towards Plymouth and raced in to Auntie Rose. 'Auntie Rose, Auntie Rose. There's a German plane coming. Look. It's ever so low.'

She came quickly out. 'Where, boy? Oh don't be daft. It's Red Cross. Look.' She pointed at the crosses on the plane. The plane was barely above us, following the railway, limping slowly along. The crew in their bubbles were clearly visible.

'It's not. It's a Dornier 17.' I knew precisely from my Dinky Toys what plane it was. 'They're German crosses. See?'

She wasn't listening. 'Look, you can see him, plain.' She waved.

'He's the gunner. Look, one engine's not working.'

'He's waving back. Wave, boy, wave. Woo-oo.'

'I think he's going to crash.'

'If they're Germans they'd shoot us.'

119

We watched it fly over the station and down the valley.

'Look, it's coming down.'

And it did. A distant explosion and a plume of smoke, just like in the pictures.

Auntie Rose put a hand to her face. 'Oh my God. D'you think they were Germans?'

'Course they were.' I was annoyed at her naivety.

'Why didn't they parachute?'

'I think they were too low.'

She was most upset. 'Those poor boys. I saw them. Young, like my Gwyn. Why didn't he shoot us if they was Germans?' She clasped me to her, too late to save me.

'I think he must've been a Saxon, one of Uncle Jack's friends.'

CHAPTER TEN

Spring unfolded into our second summer in paradise, the summer of 1941. Clearly not paradise for all, because the drift of vackies back to London had begun in spite of continued heavy air raids. The worst of the Blitz was over but there was still plenty of bombing, and more to come. Things were still going badly for our forces. We were very much in reverse, being quickly, almost contemptuously, dismissed from Greece by panzer divisions and from Crete by parachutists in preparation for Hitler's invasion of Soviet Russia. Rommel had arrived in North Africa and was driving us back to Cairo. That was the campaign that we followed avidly, poring over the maps in our atlas and in the *Daily Mirror*: Gwyn was there.

*   *   *

My life now was that of a country boy. Of course many things were different from Welling but surely most different of all was our relationship with animals. In Welling there was the odd pet and the tradesmen's horses. Here we were surrounded by all sorts of creatures: wild ones and the farm and domesticated ones.

The fish migrations were part of the rhythm of the year. When we fished for trout we would walk the banks or lie on the fallen trees over the river, spot them and—rarely in daylight and with our basic equipment—catch them; they were there all year. But the salmon peel, the local name for sea trout, much bigger and rarer, were visitors, nosing their way upstream to breed, and even harder to catch. Most spectacular and rarest of all, the migration of the eels, elvers about an inch long, filling the river and turning the shallow pools near the banks into flashing green-and-silver kaleidoscopes. They came in on the spring tides. Glass eels, they were called when very small. If you laid one on your palm you could see its organs through its flesh. There was a fish run, I suppose it was called, a channel some eight feet wide, with sluice gates, that made a bypass round the rapids just below the road bridge. We lay on our stomachs in the grass and stared into the clear water filled with countless millions of these tiny creatures swimming from—so I was told—the Sargasso Sea on the other side of the Atlantic Ocean. I went home and looked at the world atlas in the front room in wonder. How could those tiny things swim from there to here? Virtually the only other time you saw an eel was when a full-grown one all too frequently took your trout bait and you cursed the twisting, knotted, furious thing you had to get off the hook without it biting you. It often ended with your having to saw its head off and throw the two bits back into the river. We didn't eat eels, though the river was full of them, nor elvers.

We would occasionally see an otter in the river, flashing elusively through the water. 'That's the end of fishing for the day,' the locals used to say.

There was even, very rarely, a salmon to be seen in the river. When we learned of one, and if we could, we would hurry the mile or so down to the pools near the road bridge to catch a glimpse. 'Well, it was there yesterday,' the platelayer or labourer or fisherman who had seen it would tell us disappointed kids.

In summer we would go looking for adders in the woods, sometimes finding one and keeping our distance behind long sticks as we tormented it till it slid away. Our tales of ridding the woods of adders far exceeded our actions. Their poisonous bite held sway in our imaginations.

We saw rabbits daily, foxes and badgers occasionally. Moles were everywhere, but you didn't see them, only their runs and molehills, cursed by farmers and gardeners. Mrs Langdon, the teacher of the junior vackies' class, decided she would make a moleskin coat for herself so we were offered sixpence a skin. I couldn't catch a single one, though I set snares on their runs in our gardens and surrounding fields. Neither, I believe, could any vackies. For once the village kids, especially the bigger boys, showed their superiority: during dinner breaks a stream of them came to our class with skins and claimed their sixpence. I don't remember ever seeing Mrs Langdon's finished coat.

But the domestic and farm animals were the ones that engaged our attention daily and were part of our lives.

Peter, Auntie Rose's canary, brightened the day with its singing, especially when the sun got round to the window in the afternoon and struck its cage, an event which it always greeted with a burst of song. On some evenings the doors and windows were closed tight and the canary was given a free fly round the room, fluttering in a trail of feathers from picture frame to picture frame to the top of the dresser. I am not sure that the canary enjoyed these outings as much as we did. It always seemed in a panic. It was never a great problem to usher it back into its cage and sometimes we would hold it gently in our clasped hands, its anxious head darting this way and that, its tiny warm body so light and fragile-seeming, with a heart that beat fit to burst.

The cat was always locked out for these outings. The tabby that lived with us led a schizophrenic life. I loved just to touch it but it had to be constantly on guard; as far as cats were concerned Auntie Rose was unpredictable. It wasn't fed too much as it was encouraged to be a good mouser. As a result the canary was the subject of some pretty hungry glares when it sang. The cat would rub itself against Auntie Rose's leg, hopefully purring for food or milk, but if she was busy or

Auntie Rose, holding cat (not ours), and her neighbours beside the whitewashed bungalow in the Court

tripped over it you would hear, 'Oh *Duw*, get out of it,' and a kick sent the cat running. Or she would pick up a broom, in which case it became a blur as it shot out of the back door. One day I found our cat in one of the fields over the other side of the railway with a young rabbit in its mouth. It growled a warning at me as I approached in case I meant to take its prey but I had no such intention.

Our cat had, I suppose, an idyllic life compared to one unfortunate animal, victim of a vacky with an experimental turn of mind. He used to make parachutes out of handkerchiefs, tie them onto the cat and throw it out of the upstairs window. We watched fascinated as the cat hurtled through the air with the handkerchief having no effect on its descent. It would land with a thump on the grass and shoot off into the bushes with its useless equipment dragging behind it.

'I can't get the parachute to open properly, that's the trouble. I will. You see,' said the boy as he hunted for the animal and another try.

The hens in their run were something that fascinated us for only a short while on our arrival. But to collect their eggs was always a good moment. A squawking and fluttering often announced the fact that there was one to be had, or we would just have a speculative look in the coop. And there in the straw, often with bits sticking to it, still warm, better than a shop egg, was a perfect white or brown ovoid with its smooth hard shell which you could hold and wonder at before taking it in and watching Auntie Rose break it and cook it. Or perhaps she would just put it in boiling water and serve it to you in an egg cup so that you could tap it harder and harder until the end of it was a jigsaw of cracks, its beauty gone, now just something to be eaten.

We once had a lodger, a signalman. I remember coming down to breakfast and finding a boiled egg at my place, waiting to be eaten, a minor treat. I tapped at it with an anticipatory spoon and picked off the bits only to reveal that it was empty; the signalman had already eaten the contents for his breakfast and the shell had been inverted in my egg cup. There was laughter and I joined in, waiting for the genuine article to be put in its place. But there wasn't one. As I remember, Jack, Auntie Rose and the signalman were the only ones present; Uncle Jack had already gone off to work. This practical joke seems so out of character for Auntie Rose that I still wonder at it, but it happened. Perhaps it was done when her back was turned and she was trapped. An egg for breakfast wasn't that common and I felt betrayed.

Occasionally there was a chicken which was due to be eaten, a young cockerel, one too many in the run, or a hen that no longer laid. When they went broody they were put in the woodshed, I don't really know why, but they stood in there for a day or so on the logs and then were returned to the run. It seemed to work. But if one permanently stopped laying she ended up in the oven. Then it was a fight between Jack and me: we both wanted to be allowed to kill it. I cannot believe now what bloodthirsty creatures we were, but killing rabbits, chickens, any small living thing, seemed to be part of us, a treat almost. I don't think it was cruelty. We just wanted to do what the grown-ups did. It certainly involved curiosity. Anyway, Uncle Jack always did it quickly, so quickly that we barely saw it happening, though we were watching. Then the chicken was hung up on the clothes line to bleed. When Auntie Rose cleaned out its innards I remember marvelling at the tiny, half-formed, soft-shelled eggs it contained.

At one point, we had a pig in the linney. Uncle Jack brought the little piglet home one day, its head sticking out of a sack inside his jacket. It thrived and reached a good size, living on bran and kitchen waste that Auntie Rose would boil in a huge pot on the kitchen range to make swill, which smelled frightful and drove us out until the windows had been opened. Still the traces remained. Then it was time to eat the pig. A big treat in the war. A permit to kill it was required, all to do with meat rationing, and when all the red tape was done Uncle Jack prepared to hang it up by its hind legs in the linney, slit its throat and let it bleed to death. That was how it was done. Jack was allowed to help string it up but I wasn't. I was considered too young. I sat seething with disappointment in the house with Auntie Rose while Jack helped in the preparation, then he was thrown out and Uncle Jack and the Bunneys' Uncle Ned, who came over from Taphouse especially, did the deed. Auntie Rose was salting and cutting the carcass on the kitchen table for what seemed like weeks; sides of bacon seemed to hang everywhere. 'No more pigs,' she said.

*   *   *

All round us were the farms, exciting places full of activity. There were three I visited often: the Bunneys', Crago's and Treburgie, owned by the

Tamblyns, where the Burfords were billeted. At the Bunneys' we were often allowed to help in one way or another and that was good enough, to become part of that strong-smelling world, to shovel, gather, carry, round up, milk, just *do* things until you were tired, hungry and glad to go home. 'Old Bunney been getting some free labour again, has he?' would be Uncle Jack's greeting. But at Treburgie with the Burfords I remember that we played: in barns, where we could hide-and-seek and slide down chutes of straw and hay; round the pungent dung heap, which we turned over with pitchforks to envelop ourselves in the overwhelming stench of rotting straw and cow dung cleared from the milking sheds, great rich waves of it; on the tractor, excellent source of entertainment, whether still and silent as you pretended to drive it into battle against the Germans, or when you rode with Mr Tamblyn, bouncing across lumpy, bumpy fields to the roar of the motor.

But best of all were the animals. We helped drive the cattle in for milking and learned how to do it, grasping the long warm teats as instructed, pulling and squeezing and producing nothing—at first. I remember the fleshly feel of them, the massive size in my hands, almost embarrassed at the intimacy of the contact. The cow gave nothing, then little squirts of milk followed by regular full jets as you got the idea and she decided to put up with your incompetence and release her udderful, probably as relieved as you were. Mechanical milking was just coming in but even where a farm had it fitted the cows had to be finished off by hand and we were keen to do it. As you milked

128

them they chewed straw put in the stalls or just the cud. This produced prodigious quantities of wind; the noises of bovine flatulence rang round the shed, the fruitier noises often followed by the plopping of wet dung landing on concrete. Best of all was when these two events happened to one cow simultaneously. The vackies' covert grins and giggles became overt. My efforts to suppress my sniggers sometimes drew the beast's attention and she would turn and look at me with those large gentle cow's eyes, almost—to my overheated imagination—reproachful of my mirth at her loss of dignity. A cow's more-in-sorrow-than-in-anger look would reduce me to helplessness.

There were sheep to be rounded up with a companionable dog, and pigs pleased to have their backs scratched in their evil-smelling sties. Tractors had mostly replaced horses on the farms but we got the occasional ride on Crago's big farm horses.

To watch the various ponies and workhorses being shod at Uglow's the blacksmith in Dobwalls was thrilling and a bit frightening. There is an awful lot of horse when you get close to one, especially when you are a smallish eight-year-old. Cows look at you with trust, but horses look at you suspiciously. And with good reason. Each new shoe was heated in the furnace till it was red-hot, then, while malleable, beaten and bent to the right size, plunged into cold water to cool it just enough before it was fitted to the hoof, hissing and smelling of burning hoof and horsehair as it was nailed on. Although this was painless for the horses, they did not care for the business, not surprisingly. They stirred uneasily and laid back their ears as they smelled themselves scorching. Occasionally the more spirited or nervous ones would lash out. Mr Uglow would dodge the kick, swear, pick up the red-hot shoe with tongs and start again.

On Saturday mornings we could earn pocket money from local farmers by herding pigs, sheep and cattle into the pens in Doublebois goods yard by Blamey and Morgan's mill. The thrill of being partially responsible for getting the animals down a mile or two of lanes without them diving through a hedge or running off somewhere was enormous. The difficult bit was when we left the road and had to get them into the pens without them escaping across the goods yard and on to the main line, a disaster that rarely happened. We stood in a row with arms spread, holding sticks and making noises, yet still some independent-minded animal would dash through our line and make a break for it. Difficult for a boy to stop a full-grown cow, or even a pig, once it has made up its mind. The sheep you could grapple with, hanging on to their wool. Once a goods train coming up the line from the valley was brought to a halt as the main line was dotted with men and boys trying to usher a lowing, terrified steer away from a very messy end, back to the one planned for it. One Saturday we had a very randy pig who tried to mount every other pig of whatever sex that was in its pen. We boys were delighted and urged it on, amazed at its pink wriggling corkscrew penis. The pig finally made the mistake of climbing onto one of its companions at the wrong end and got its penis bitten. It ran squealing round the pen, barging the others aside in its agony while we chortled with

130

glee. Once all the animals were in, we swung on the rails round the pens, slapping the pigs and cows like knowledgeable farmers, complacent in the skill we had shown and each with a sixpence in his pocket.

CHAPTER ELEVEN

One day Jack and I joined Ken and Elsie Plummer behind the row of outside privies that sat across the foot of the gardens of Railway Cottages: a raid on Granny Peters' gooseberry bushes. Scrumping was to us vackies an occupation of our childhood, to the village kids it was unknown. It just didn't seem to have occurred to them, or perhaps they were used to taking what they wanted. Nor did we vackies do it because we were hungry for fruit, or greedy. There were all sorts of wild fruit and nuts in the woods, fields and hedgerows all round us. No, it was simply something we did. Granny Peters was Jimmy Peters' grandmother, which might explain why he didn't feel inclined to rob her. She was, to us, half funny, half witch and lived in the Court at number 4. Her gooseberry bushes were laden with golden hairy goosegogs.

Jack and Ken were in charge of our raiding party, planning it with military precision. 'Look, Ken, it's best if Elsie keeps watch here and we crawl across the paths.'

Ken agreed, holding just enough reserve in his tone to show that he was joint leader, not second-in-command. 'Yes. I vote for that.'

Elsie had her own ideas. 'I want to come with

131

you.'

'You can't,' Ken said.

'Why?'

'Because you're useless.'

'You're mean you are, you sod.'

'You always make a noise or get seen or something.'

'I can't help it if people notice me.'

Ken sighed. 'She makes me sick.'

This routine family spat over, we got on with the serious business. Jack resumed. 'Well, Terry's the smallest. He can get right in under the prickles and pass out the goosegogs.'

I was glad of my important role. 'Yeah, no one will see me.'

'Then you and me, Ken, can get round the back there and get all them there.'

'OK.'

'And Elsie can stay by the corner and see all the windows and if anybody comes to the bogs.'

Elsie was indignant. 'I'm not staying here, it smells.'

'Stop moaning or we won't give you any,' Ken threw in.

'Don't want any.'

I suppose any plan which included an unwilling Elsie in a vital role was doomed, but Jack ignored this. 'All right, come on. Terry first.' We wriggled round the odorous privies on our stomachs with an excess of secrecy that would have excited attention from a mile away. We boys slid in among the bushes while Elsie kept watch and communed with her changing body.

In the cocoon of the gooseberry bushes it was both cosy and painful. No matter how careful I was, they pricked.

Jack whispered, 'Come on, Terry. Pass 'em out.'

Ken could see me. 'He's eating 'em.'

They were delicious. 'I only had a few,' I said.

Suddenly there was a distant female voice calling, very Cornish, very old: Granny Peters. 'Hey, you. You boys. What you to?'

Ken saw her first. 'Oh no. That's her.'

'What b'you doin' in there?'

Jack turned on Ken. 'Where's your cousin?'

'She's gone.'

Granny Peters was on top of us now. 'Why be you lying down there?'

In my anxiety to get out, my clothes were impaled on the barbs. Gooseberries in my pockets were squashed as I struggled. Ken ran for it; Jack stayed with me. Granny Peters stood over us, a figure to frighten you from sleep.

*   *   *

That evening in 7 Railway Cottages Jack and I were standing in the dock, in the court of Auntie Rose and Uncle Jack, an intimidating tribunal. Uncle Jack opened the proceedings. 'So you two tried to steal Granny Peters' gooseberries, did you?'

We were silent.

'Well, did you?'

'We were only scrumping,' I mumbled miserably.

'What's that, then? Cockney for stealing?'

'Scrumping is when it's apples and things,' said Jack helpfully.

'I know what it is.'

Auntie Rose joined in. 'I'll never hold up my head in the Court again. Ashamed, I am of you both. Poor old Granny Peters.'

Our heads drooped further.

Uncle Jack stared at us. 'What are we going to do with you?'

We didn't know, but Auntie Rose did. 'You're going to go in to her and say you're sorry, to start with. And you take her in some of my rock cakes.'

'Yes, Auntie Rose.'

'You know she do make jam from all her fruit and she earns her money from it and she do give us a jar every Christmas. And then you steal 'em.'

Uncle Jack was as unforgiving. 'If you wanted some gooseberries why didn't you ask? Were you hungry? Don't we feed you?'

More shuffled feet.

'You take my rock cakes and you go in there and you ask her what jobs you can do for her.'

We knocked timidly on Granny Peters' door. No answer. 'Perhaps she's out,' I said hopefully to Jack, ready to run.

'She's never out.' He knocked louder. 'Granny Peters? Granny Peters?'

Suddenly she was there before us. I am not sure how old she was, certainly the oldest inhabitant of Doublebois, though the trio in 1 Railway Cottages at the opposite end from us, an elderly man and his two sisters about whom there were incestuous defamatory rumours, must have run her close. Her voice was cracked, barely of this world, she wheezed; she wasn't really there in one sense, though with the support of her relatives near by and the neighbours she managed. 'Who's tha'?'

'Jack and Terry, Granny Peters, the boys from

134

Auntie Rose's.'

'Oh, the vackies. Aaah. Hallo, my boodies.'

'We brought you some of her rock cakes.'

Granny Peters took us in, talking wheezily all the time. 'Aun'ee Rose. Oooh. Her rock cakes. Aaah. Give 'em here. I'll soak they in my tea. You boys be from Lunnen, eh? I was there once, with my Arthur. Too many 'osses. Everywhere. 'Osses all round you. Worse'n Plymouth, 'twas.' She gestured to me. 'Come yere, my pretty. Come closer.'

I was rigid. 'Oh no.'

'Go on,' urged Jack, in no danger.

'She smells funny,' I whispered as I submitted to an embrace of old person's smells.

'Oh, you'm pretty 'n no mistake. Don't wriggle, I won't hurt 'ee. You mind me o' my Billy. Ginger, they call 'ee. All down Dobwalls Street they chanted, "Ginger, you'm barmy, you oughtta join the army," 'n he did.'

To my horror she started to cry.

Jack tried to interrupt. 'Auntie Rose said—'

'Oh Billy, my firstborn, my pretty, where you to now? South Africa, he went, and the Boers shot 'ee. There's his medals. He warn't simple. The army took him. So he couldn't a' bin, could 'ee? They maids led him on. 'Twas they fault, not 'ee. He didn't hurt they. You wouldn't hurt a fly, would you, my pretty?'

I struggled in folds of enveloping cloth. 'She won't let me go.'

'Don't worry. I think she's all right.'

'His father, he was the simple one. I 'ad eight from 'ee. All gone to God. He took 'n all: three in the war; two when they was little like you, my

135

boody. Henry, he went on the railway. Working on the line. Down the valley. They threw a bottle from a train and it hit his lovely face. Oh. The 4.12 to Snozzle, 'twas.' (All locals pronounced St Austell like that.) 'Oh, I outlived all my own children. 'Tis not natural. 'Tis wonderful lonely.'

'Isn't Jimmy Peters' dad your son?' asked Jack.

'Oh yes. Yes. I forgot 'ee. Huh. I don't count 'ee. He's still here.'

I tried a new tack. 'If you let me go, I'll take your jug and get some water from the pump.'

'Wha' for? 'Tis half full.'

'Auntie Rose said we got to.'

'Oh, Auntie Rose. Yes. Her rock cakes: they'm well named.'

Jack got to the point. 'And we're sorry we tried to steal your gooseberries.'

'You want some gooseberries? Go on, then. They be yansome now. Take that bowl and bring me some. I'll make you some jam. Yere, come yere, little one. Let me touch your hair.'

'I got to go. Auntie Rose is calling.'

'Give me a kiss, Billy. Henry, give your mam a kiss 'fore you go to work.'

But we were out of the door with jug and bowl.

'We'll bring you some gooseberries in this bowl, Granny Peters.'

'Come on, quick.'

And we were gone, her ethereal, quavering voice floating behind us, still echoing in my head to this day.

*　　　　*　　　　*

Elsie Plummer was a very good girl.

She went to church on Sunday
To pray to God to give her strength
To kiss the boys on Monday.

In our tiny community we all knew each other's characters very well. There was no escape. Elsie had her reputation, she had worked hard enough for it, but I don't know whether our liaison was known about or not. I never got teased about it so perhaps it wasn't; one secret she managed to keep. Perhaps it was just too unlikely. With my first winter in Cornwall over we met again and again in the house in the woods as I grew more and more jealous of her and confused about my own feelings. I was nowhere near puberty.

'Terry, let's play families.'

'No.'

'Oh, go on. You be Dad and I'll be Mam.' By now she had learned from the cinema what to say and how to say it. She threw herself into the scenarios she had invented for us. 'I love you, Dad. You can tell. Listen to my heart.' She paused at my lack of response, entirely due to inhibition. 'Feel it.' I could do it only half-heartedly. 'No, inside. Undo them, can't you?'

'Don't want to.'

'You do.'

'You're older'n me.'

'I'm fourteen.'

'I'm eight. Boys should be older'n girls.'

'Who said?'

'They always are.'

'Not. Mrs Kitto's older'n Mr Kitto. By miles.'

'How d'you know?'

'The whole village knows. So's all right. I like

137

you best. You're the youngest.' She tried her new-found seductive tone again. 'Have you seen my new knickers?'

'Everybody has.'

She was indignant. 'When?'

'When you do high kicks.'

'Like this?' She lay back and demonstrated, foot high in the air.

I was non-committal as I covertly looked.

'Want to see 'em now?'

'I just did.'

She leant close to me. 'Want to touch?'

I was routed. 'Don't know.'

'You knew the other day.'

'Shut up.'

'You want to, really.'

'I'm going.'

'You're scared.'

At last it burst out of me. 'Just stop talking about it all the time.'

She understood at once. 'Sorry,' she said quickly. 'Sorry, sorry. Yere. Lie down. By me. I won't speak again. Promise.'

I did as she asked.

'That's right,' she breathed in relief. 'Give me your hand.'

CHAPTER TWELVE

The soldiers stationed in Doublebois House were always being replaced. When we first arrived in Cornwall it was occupied by the men I have described, shocked after the Dunkirk debacle.

138

They soon moved on and the place was taken over by a succession of different regiments, generally under training for some event or other. At one point Canadians were briefly there and suddenly left. We read in the papers a few days later of the ill-fated raid on Dieppe in which so many Canadians died. Doublebois seemed to go into unofficial mourning for a while.

Every time we got wind of a change of personnel, if we weren't at school we children would all run into the Park and hang from the beech tree, cheering and waving, excited by all the activity. The soldiers always waved back and were often singing—dirty songs if we were lucky. Sometimes they were marched out to the station and boarded a waiting train. Then we would all run back down the Court and hang over the wire fence behind the wash-house, waving them out of sight up the line. Generally the movement was by road. Soldiers we knew, guards who had let us see their rifles and examine their equipment, went riding away in lorries, waving and smiling, always those two actions. Sometimes the replacements came riding in at the same time as the previous incumbents were leaving, so there seemed to be a frenzy of activity with a military policeman directing traffic at the crossroads. As convoys of lorries roared past the end of the Court, it became hazardous even to venture onto the normally empty A38. Nevertheless, we always dashed across it to the Park to watch the newcomers drive in through the left-hand gate and up that drive as the others departed by the right.

But most often and gloriously, one contingent would leave and there would be nobody there for a few days or weeks. The whole estate became an empty adventure playground for us children, vackies and locals. The two drives up to the big house were lined with rhododendrons and other shrubs. Between the drives was a monkey puzzle tree, beloved of the Victorians who had built this place. We couldn't climb it and soon gave up trying. There were woods and empty Nissen huts to explore; there was an abandoned swimming pool, full of accumulated water, beside which I spent hours watching tadpoles and newts in spring, and water boatmen making lazy circles on the still surface during lazy summer afternoons. We pushed out little boats made of leaves and twigs with ants as the crews, we trailed our hands, we saw a snake trapped in there one day, swimming anxiously round and round looking for a way out, keeping us at bay, but it was only a grass snake, I think, gone the next day.

Our glittering prize in the middle of all this was the big house, now empty and at our mercy. Easy entry through a broken window and there was an unoccupied, echoing manor for our playground. We made full use of it, crashing and banging about until the owner of the estate, old Mr Steer, known to us as Old Man Steer, would appear to drive us briefly out. But his heart wasn't in it after the soldiers' destructive occupation. We soon returned. He lived in Home Farm, behind the big house, looking out over the valley, alone, I think, or with a housekeeper, because he still worked the farm.

In the lodge by the right-hand entrance of the twin drives up to Doublebois House lived Mr and Mrs Holman. Mrs Holman was the daughter or

140

granddaughter, I'm not sure which, of Old Man Steer. Mr Holman was a solicitor who commuted daily to Plymouth to practise. They were a gentle, childless couple in their late thirties or early forties who made a point of befriending us vackies. They formed a mixed scout or cub group for all the children of Doublebois and we met in their house and played Kim's Game, which I loved and still do, did first aid, read books on tree, bird and insect recognition and went on patrols round the estate.

Best of all, Mr Holman, a keen fisherman, took Jack and me on some all-night trout-fishing trips on the river during the school holidays. The thrill of being allowed to do such a thing, of having the responsibility of staying awake all night, was considerable. The actual event involved a walk in the late-evening light; we were full of anticipation, following a footpath down the hill from the back of the estate to the river, loaded with a borrowed rod each, bait, sandwiches, wet gear, a blanket, drinks and a torch. This was followed by long hours of just sitting on the bank in the dark with rod and line, often bored, often frightened of the noises in the pitch-black woods that surrounded us. Sometimes these noises came, mysteriously, from the river itself, sudden splashes that could not have been caused by the flow: perhaps fish, perhaps an otter, perhaps something else in our overheated imaginations.

We broke the night up with sandwiches and hot drinks from a Thermos. Occasionally your line jumped from a bite and all was excitement. It was generally an eel to throw back or kill if the hook was too far down. By torchlight we pushed squirming worms longways onto the hooks for bait and caught the odd trout or three which went into our keep net. I never worked out how the fish saw the worms in the dark; perhaps they smelled them. Up we would trudge in the early-morning light, leave Mr Holman, go home to gut our catch, watch Auntie Rose fry them for breakfast, eat them and fall into bed as Mr Holman got the morning train to his office in Plymouth. In spite of all the fright, cold and boredom I was always eager to be asked again.

*   *   *

Another all-night thrill, which happened to me only twice I think, was to be allowed—again in the holidays—to do the night shift in the signal box of the next section down the line, Largan box. The signalmen in the box on Doublebois station were local and permanent. Jimmy Peters' dad was one at some point. Three miles down the line, controlling the next section, was a box right in the heart of the Fowey Valley, deep in the woods, a few yards from the river. These signalmen were not local, only temporary, often taking lodgings in one or other of Railway Cottages. The shifts were 10 p.m. to 6 a.m., 6 a.m. to 2 p.m., 2 p.m. to 10 p.m. We were often allowed in the box on the station but it was an event to be allowed to go down to the other box. It was far enough to demand that we had to be accompanied there and back on the line. So it meant an entire shift with the signalman. One summer's evening I went down and spent from 10 p.m. to 6 a.m. in the box.

It was quite different from the fishing experience. The noise of the nearby river was a soothing background outside the safety of the dimly lit box. On that warm summer's night it became a focus for every moth in the woods. They fluttered in and flopped down round the oil lamp and hovered and mated and died by the hundred. The few trains, nearly all goods, were in mid-rush down the valley or trying to gain speed for the climb, so clattered swiftly past the box with a wave from the driver and fireman, who you could see in the light from the locomotive's furnace. Another wave from the guard, who could see us but who was just a shadow. I was allowed to heave on the great heavy signal levers, nearly as tall as me, and to ring the warning bells to the next section. In the long silences between the trains we saw owls float soundlessly down the line. Sometimes, their eyes turned towards us, just caught gleaming yellow in the far limits of our light, we saw foxes and badgers—lions and tigers in my imagination— crossing, vulnerable for a few yards on the rails before the undergrowth swallowed them. After the sun rose and came shining down the line there was the three-mile walk in the early-morning light, straight into its beams, back up the track to Doublebois, breakfast and bed.

*   *   *

After one of the empty intervals, soldiers once more descended on Doublebois. The Big House was requisitioned and overflowed. The Nissen huts were reoccupied. Girls took to walking the lanes near by with increasing frequency; Elsie, now abundantly fifteen, lost interest in me. If the vackies had shocked nearby Dobwalls, the soldiers

143

stunned it. As lorries trundled along the main road their bawdy songs rang out:

> Hitler has only got one ball.
> Goering has two but very small.
> Himmler has something similar
> And poor old Goebbels has no balls at all.

The Miss Polmanors of the village rushed to the Methodist minister. 'Mr Buckroyd, Mr Buckroyd, have you heard—'
'Yes, yes,' and then wearily, 'There's a war on.'

*   *   *

Camp concerts were huge events. Entertainment was at a premium in our backwater. The locals—and especially the children—did their best to get places. Professional entertainers and the Looe Fishermen's Choir performed in the long Nissen hut that was the camp canteen. I remember one concert in particular. The compere, dressed as a vicar, made an announcement that brought a shout of laughter and left me puzzled: 'I should like to apologise to Mr Shorthouse for misspelling his name in the parish magazine.' What's funny about that? When I had made the connection I thought for days about how rude and clever it was: not just one possible subversive answer, but two.

After the choir a sing-song, 'You Are My Sunshine'. Rows of soldiers and not enough girls sang with a sudden, rolling, bellowing roar and swayed as they sang. The force and enthusiasm of all those open male throats gave that song an emotional power the composer could only have dreamed of. Oh, my wartime childhood: the stinging smoke and sickly beer smell; the distant light on the stage; and here in the comforting dark, rows of soldiers and the meagre ration of girls.

It was my childhood but it was their youth: hands tight round willing waists; male fingers pressing into thin summer frocks; female cheeks against harsh Army tunics; bawling out their fervour for the moment with a passion I could sense but not comprehend. Their passion was not to get at the Germans, of course, but to stay—for ever if possible—in the warm half-dark, in the promise of a smile and against the pressure of another body that might be snatched away. They had the threat of extinction to sharpen their senses.

*   *   *

We kids hung round the soldiers constantly, cadging rides, holding their rifles, wearing their forage caps and, when the sentries allowed us to, swinging open the big iron gates at the entrances to the drives of Doublebois House so that cars, lorries and even Bren Carriers could rumble in and out. Then we could swing the twelve-foot-long things closed again with a satisfying clang. The gates were deemed by the military too much of a bother constantly to open and close so were taken off their hinges and leant against the wall to be removed. Instead of swinging them we just sat on them.

The smallest of us all was Teddy Camberwell, a five-year-old, evacuated with his mother and baby sister. He was not one of us Welling crowd. I call him Teddy Camberwell, but I don't remember his surname, just that he was bombed out from Camberwell in the Blitz. Teddy, his mother and little sister were billeted at 3 Railway Cottages and he tagged along with us in most of our play. On this day he was at the end of a row of us sitting on the gate when a lorry came round the corner, caught the gate, tipped it forward and left us falling backwards into the bushes—except for Teddy. He was thrown forward and went under the gate. And the gate went under the lorry.

I clambered out and looked at the scene before me: the driver, staring aghast at the result of his tiny error; the unbelieving sentry; three other children, one with his hand in his mouth, all beyond tears; Teddy's crushed body under the gate, leaking blood and other things. I turned and ran for the only help I trusted. 'Auntie Rose, Auntie Rose. Come quickly, Teddy Camberwell's dead. He's dead. Teddy Camberwell's dead.'

I arrived at our house at the far end of the Court as Auntie Rose emerged. She stared at me, shocked. 'You're covered in blood.' This was nothing, just scratches from the bushes I had landed in.

'Teddy Camberwell's dead.'

'What are you talking about?'

'A lorry went over the gate.'

We ran back up to the main road. The sentry, accompanied by the bemused driver and three children, was walking up the main road carrying Teddy's tiny, crumpled body to his home at 3 Railway Cottages.

Auntie Rose shouted at them. 'What are you doing? What are you doing, man?'

'Are you the mother?' asked the sentry, probably dreading the answer.

'No, where are you taking him?'

'The boys said he lives in the cottages, here.'

'What are you trying to do? Give his mother a present, you bloody fool? Take him back to the camp.'

The sentry, no more than a teenager, was hopelessly out of his depth. 'I didn't know where to—'

Auntie Rose practically pushed him. 'Go on. Take him to your medical officer. His mother'll be out any minute.' She turned to me. 'You, into the wash-house and get that blood off you. You, Jimmy and Brian, home and tell your mams. Alan, go home and get Miss Laity to come to my house.' Alan was billeted with the district nurse.

I next saw Auntie Rose taking Teddy's mother into our house, where she lay collapsed and sobbing on the sofa, watched by Jack's and my detached, curious eyes until we were driven out. So much emotion seemed more than one person could contain. Her body jerked and heaved as her grief tore its way out of her.

The next day a soldier appeared in the Court: a private, Teddy's father. He was accompanied by an awkward-looking Army padre, an officer, and stood mutely, arms pinned to his side by his wife as she clung to him and sobbed anew. What guilt she must have suffered besides her simple agony. To have brought her son to Cornwall for safety and then to have this news for his father. Auntie Rose had already washed, dressed and laid out Teddy, something she was experienced in, so I was later told, from her days in the mining village in South

147

Wales.

One day later, Jack and I, Jimmy Peters, Brian Bunney, Harold Packham and Ken Plummer were to carry Teddy's coffin to the station to put it on the 9 a.m. Cornish Riviera express to Paddington: a farewell gesture from us all. The train was stopped especially. A makeshift military band from the camp was to lead us. The whole of Doublebois came out to watch. A funeral march was considered inappropriate for so small a child, so some genius of military bandsmanship used his discretion and 'Early One Morning' rang tinnily out as we carried the tiny coffin from 3 Railway Cottages to the station, followed by Teddy's father and mother carrying his oblivious baby sister.

Because I was the smallest boy, I was one of the two in the middle. My shoulders weren't high enough so I had to hold my hands up to reach the coffin. The couple of hundred yards to the station seemed endless. Teddy's coffin was not long enough to accommodate three boys a side and nobody had taught us to walk in step and, as we tripped and shuffled along, my heels and calves were skinned by the hobnail boots of the boys behind as I inflicted similar injuries on the boy in front, whose heels were meanwhile gashing my shins. Mr Rawlings the stationmaster, stout and self-important, held the train as we filed down the slope of Station Approach between two rows of soldiers presenting reversed arms.

Passengers stared from the train as we clumsily put Teddy in the smelly guard's van, on to straw that was laid for some tethered creature, a calf or goat, which stirred uneasily at the activity round it.

The train departed and we turned and ran hard

148

to our schools in Dobwalls over a mile away, each to our different classes. I was the only one in Junior Vackies. Because I was good at my lessons I was one of Mrs Langdon's favourites. But my habit of arriving late in the morning and returning late from lunch because of games and digressions with the bigger boys had gone too far this time.

She stared sternly at me. 'Terry Frisby, you're late again.'

All I could produce was heavy breathing.

'What is your excuse this time?'

I couldn't utter.

'Look at the time. And your legs. All scratched and bloody. What have you been doing? Fighting? Climbing?'

'No, Miss,' I managed.

'Forty minutes you're late. This is a record, I think.'

One of the vackies who lived at Treburgie Farm near Doublebois put her hand up. 'Please, Miss. Miss.'

'Be quiet, June Burford. Terry, come here.'

The dreaded ruler was produced. God knows how such a failure of communication had occurred in our gossip-ridden little community but Mrs Langdon in Dobwalls somehow knew nothing of the Doublebois farewell ceremony. I got six whacks across my knuckles and broke into breathless sobs. It had all finally got to me.

Mrs Langdon was not a liberal wielder of the ruler and probably didn't feel that happy herself. 'Now go to your place and don't be late again.'

June didn't give up. 'Please, Miss.'

'Be quiet, June.'

My sobs grew louder.

149

'And stop snivelling, Terry. You've had that much before and earned it.'

'*Please*, Miss.' June's arm was straining for the ceiling.

Mrs Langdon turned rattily to her. '*Yes*. What *is* it, June?'

'Please, Miss. He's been carrying Teddy Camberwell's coffin. They put it on the train this morning at Doublebois.'

CHAPTER THIRTEEN

The Bunney children's Uncle Ned drove a lorry for Blamey and Morgan. In school holidays, Blamey and Morgan's mill was a magnet for us. You could slide down chutes built for sacks of grain, rope them together and help wind them out of first-floor loading bays into the lorry, sit in piles of loose grain or cow cake and run it through your hands as you sank into it. There were a hundred other ways we could supposedly help in this busy workplace as long as we behaved ourselves and the men tolerated us, or until we were ordered out by authority, or—sad days—not allowed in at all.

Trips with the Bunneys' Uncle Ned were the best of all as he delivered produce to the farms in the area. The Bunney children had priority; he could get two, or perhaps three, in the cab with him, so we others had to hang about and hope. Occasionally, depending on the load, the bigger boys could ride in the back, clinging to the sacks as the lorry wove its way through the empty roads and lanes. Meeting another vehicle was rare, just tractors, district nurse Laity—she had both a car and a bike—and the occasional piece of military hardware: a Bren Carrier, a dispatch rider, a Land-Rover and, later, jeeps. After the loads were delivered we could all stand in the empty back, holding on to the frame attached to the cab, the wind in our hair, shouting and singing songs that were blown away, waving madly at anyone we saw.

One day Ned took a bend a bit sharply, hit a bump at the same time and the oldest Bunney, David, shot into the air out of the lorry and over the hedge. Frightened, we beat on top of the cab and shouted. The lorry pulled up, we told Ned and all of us raced back to the bend. We peered through and over the hedge. No David. As we searched we heard a shout from down the road beyond the lorry and there was David clambering over a gate. He had run across the field after us, afraid he would be left behind. A bush had broken his fall and he had nothing more than the scratches we could see and the odd bruise. I don't remember his uncle's reaction but he must have been mightily relieved. We all crammed into the cab for the rest of the journey home and later boasted madly about the incident, exaggerating whenever possible. Lorry rides ceased for the remainder of that holiday, to be continued later.

The lorry took us to many farms that merge into one in my memory except when we went across the moor. Bodmin Moor in its many moods I remember with clarity, almost awe. We went as far as Jamaica Inn on the A30, a name that held a unique place in our imagination; we expected to see smugglers and Excise men, disappointed with the farm labourers and occasional travelling salesmen who were in the bar while Ned had a pint and we stood outside with crisps or pop if we were lucky. We stopped at Dozmary Pool, supposedly bottomless, and stared at its surface, dark under the scudding clouds, and at the sedge, the gorse, the tufty grass that made up the forbidding landscape round it.

Dozmary Pool had a legend that we all knew well: Giant Tredegor had made a pact with the Devil. He sold his soul in exchange for riches in his lifetime. After his death the Devil gave him the task of emptying Dozmary Pool with a limpet shell with a hole in it. This task to last until he succeeded or for eternity. Every so often Giant Tredegor grew fed up with this and tried to run away across the moor. The Devil would send his hounds after him to bring him back and if you listened carefully you could hear them howling. You could recognise this howling, we were told, because it sounded like the wind moaning in telephone wires—only there were no telephone wires on the moor. When we were out of the lorry we listened and, sure enough, there was the sound we had been told to expect. It must have been the wind soughing through the grass and round the rocks. We would climb back into the lorry, enjoyably scared, and look back at the cheerless stretch of water, glad to be leaving.

We were also told that Dozmary Pool was the place where King Arthur threw Excalibur and the hand came out, caught it and waved it three times before disappearing. But looking at the place I couldn't really make that connection; it was simply too bleak, free of Arthurian or any sort of romance. It was Giant Tredegor running from the

Devil's hounds that caught my imagination. Every time I walked the roads or lanes round Doublebois and heard the wind in the telephone wires I pictured the whole thing and looked over my shoulder.

The moor was generally bleak, always menacing, or when low sullen clouds reigned, even dreary—it caught every weather front coming in off the Atlantic. But on a rare fine day it could be magnificent. The horizon stretched away, wild flowers blew in the eternal south-westerlies, the grass welcomed you to lie down in the sun. On such days there were plovers and lapwings, ravens, rooks and buzzards wheeling, distant rabbits who disappeared before you could blink, even shyer than the farmland rabbits we were always hunting. And, especially, there were larks everywhere, rising from the heather before us with their hysterical, cascading song. There was a story, often repeated to us complete with accent, about a cockney vacky, who, on first seeing and hearing a lark hovering and singing, pointed to it and said to his teacher, 'Look, Miss, there's a sparrer up there. He can't go up and he can't go down and 'ee ain't 'arf 'ollering.'

I wasn't aware then how much it all affected me. When I returned to the moor years later I could feel my former childish joy rising in me again.

*　　　*　　　*

In our first spring in Cornwall, I am sorry to say, we often went bird's-nesting, unlike the local boys, although I don't remember that we were a terrible scourge of the local avian population. Nor do I

153

remember ever taking or blowing eggs, not because of any scruples but because it didn't interest me, though I saw some blown and wondered how it could be done. Often broken eggs lay on the ground under the nests: lovely, tiny, delicate, shattered worlds. That was how you and (more serious for the birds) the cats often found them. Though even when the cats had found a nest, they generally couldn't get to it because of the foliage and us chasing them away. When left alone they just crouched below, waiting while the parents went about their business. The cats' only chance would be an unwary fledgling in a week or two's time.

What appealed to me was to find a nest with eggs and return to see them hatched: scrawny, bald, ugly little chicks with gaping beaks into which we put worms or insects while the anxious parents fluttered and scolded us from nearby bushes. We were soon told not to do that as the parents would abandon their chicks if they were fed by someone else. I have never really established whether this old country saw is true but such sayings are generally based on fact. The wild, naked, vulnerable scraps had none of the appeal of the day-old chicks that appeared in our chicken run every spring: fluffy, Disney objects that touched all hearts before they grew big enough to lay if they were hens or go into the pot if they weren't. The wild-bird chicks developed down, then feathers and were soon perched on a twig or on the clothes line in the garden, or on farm buildings in a row before they challenged gravity. Songbirds were all round us; we didn't need to go down to the woods to find their nests—although we sometimes did—

they were in every bush and hedgerow.

But buzzards were different. Buzzards were big, nested in inaccessible places and their eggs were prized. If you got one it proved that you had dared and achieved something.

Ken and Eric Plummer, Jack and I set off one day for the quarry. A buzzard had been seen circling there. It was the right time of year, there must be a nest somewhere. The quarry was down the main road, past the Rabbit Field and on the right, just where the woods started, a great chunk which had been blown out of the hillside bit by bit to get the slate. When they were blasting, which wasn't often, we were forbidden to go near it; notices were put out on the main road and traffic was held up until a satisfying boom was heard and it could go through.

We crouched way down in the quarry and searched the sheer faces and steps of slate above us. It didn't take long. A buzzard wheeled in and settled on the bough of a stunted tree near the top of the quarry. There was the nest, a ramshackle affair of sticks and bits, in the tree. The other bird was sitting. It soon took off and the first one took its place. We set off round the quarry and up the hill through the woods until we were near where the nest should be. We crept through the undergrowth to the edge of the quarry and peered about us. There was the nest with the bird on it. It hadn't seen us. One of the Plummers found a broken branch and we stripped it of twigs. We crept nearer. She saw us and stirred uneasily.

Ken, the older Plummer, crept forward with his long stick and prodded at the bird. He could barely reach her. The tree hung out over the quarry. The bird briefly pecked at the stick, but was soon intimidated. Reluctantly it shuffled to its feet and took off, falling away on a glide before it languorously flapped its way up and out of sight. In the nest, snugly lined with moss and leaves, lay three glorious buzzard's eggs, white with brownish veins or marks, a little smaller than hen's eggs.

The problem was: how to get them? The tree bent alarmingly when we tested our weight on it; we didn't want to tip them out; the ground was a long way below for either eggs or boy to fall to. The solution was obvious from the first: as always, I was the smallest and lightest. We made a chain, Ken anchored himself to a tree and I slid out along the branch, which creaked beneath me. I reached out with one hand but couldn't make it. Bits of earth and loose stones rattled down the slates below me. I looked down into the quarry and clung tighter to the tree, reducing my reach. I tried again and could just reach an egg by all of us moving forward in our chain. I heard the slithering of heels in the ground behind me as I strained for the nearest egg. I got it and was passing it back when there were shouts and consternation. The furious buzzards had returned together, mewing and flapping. Nearly dropping me and the egg into the quarry the others dragged me back and we all fled. You don't realise it until you are close up, but a buzzard's wingspan is about a yard and a half and its beak looks enormous when coming at you.

We proudly showed our prize to Uncle Jack. He was unimpressed. 'Oh, what did you want to do that for? They're not harming you. They're on our side, the buzzards. They eat rabbits and moles and rats. Put it back and leave 'em alone in future.'

156

Abashed, we wondered what to do. Uncle Jack's disapproval meant less to the Plummer boys than to us but nobody prized the egg any more. They shrugged the matter off and walked away. As for Uncle Jack, he couldn't possibly have known what risks his casual 'Put it back' involved Jack and me in. We made our resolution: the next day we went down to the quarry, frightened away the sitting bird and, once more, I slid out along the tree, insecurely held by Jack, and replaced the egg. Just as well I didn't slip; he would have had to let go or come with me. I don't believe the egg could possibly have hatched; we probably knew that at the time, but it seemed like atonement.

We went and watched out for the buzzard chicks to hatch but couldn't really be sure as we were soon back to school after the Easter holidays, chastened and cured of bird's-nesting. When I think now of the risks we took then and on numerous other occasions, as we ran free and wild in the Cornish countryside, it seems a miracle to me that of all us vackies only little Teddy Camberwell met his premature end there.

* * *

Putting ha'pennies on the rail before a train went through was something we all tried; the incentive, apart from experimental curiosity, was to turn a ha'penny into a penny. After the train had gone over it, it was certainly twice the size but you could never pass it off as a penny or use it again as a ha'penny. We soon desisted from this expensive pastime.

Shunting in the goods yard went on all the time.

We often tried to join in. We knew the porters, guards and the men on the footplate of the various tank engines. If they were in the right mood we could throw the points levers, run beside the rolling wagons, pull the brakes on and even go on the footplate. But the sight of the stationmaster walking down the slope off the end of the platform, across the main line and under the bridge towards us, meant that we quickly vanished and the men wouldn't let us near again for a while, clearly having been told off. When there was no shunting and the stationmaster was off duty we played among the stationary goods wagons at will. If we could find one that was well down the siding out of the way we took turns to lie down under it between the rails and, using a shunting pole, roll it over the boy on the ground to prove the point that a train could go right over you without hurting you. There were many stories of people having saved themselves from being killed by doing just that, hurling themselves down under sixty-mile-an-hour expresses and walking away unscathed. Our games with the goods wagon were a preparation for one of us to do that on the main line one day. We stood beside the line and, with heightened senses because of our project, examined at close hand the massive rush and roar that a speeding train makes as it thunders by. Nobody volunteered to go first. The thought of the major trouble you would be in if you survived was as much a deterrent as the prospect of a mangled death.

During the war all road signposts and signs identifying stations were removed so that, in the words of the man on Welling station, 'The Germans won't know where they are when they get here.' The stationmaster Mr Rawlings would promenade up and down the platform whenever a train pulled in saying, 'Doublebois,' with an upward inflexion, followed by, 'Doublebois,' on a downward. He did this very quietly. When a 4-6-0 Hall-class or Grange-class engine was letting off steam, having climbed the bank from the valley, his little melody, 'Doublebois,' up, 'Doublebois,' down, was completely inaudible. People would lean out and ask where they were when only a foot or two from him. This gave great pleasure to Dad when he visited, who compared him to the man at Eltham Park, two stations from Welling, who, over a silently arriving electric train, would bawl, with the second word on two wavering notes, 'Elt-ham Pa-a-rk,' so that he could be heard across the whole of Eltham in the blackout.

*   *   *

During our school holidays we were taken by Auntie Rose—and sometimes Uncle Jack if he was on his fortnight summer break—on outings, always with packed lunches and bottles of pop. The trips I remember best were to Looe, the most frequent destination. After that came Polperro, Newquay and Padstow. All were by train, with our privilege tickets reducing the cost because Auntie Rose and Uncle Jack were a railway couple and we were railway children. Dad would sign vouchers and send them to Auntie Rose and we would go down to Doublebois station and present our Southern Railway credentials to the ticket clerk in this heart of the Great Western Railway empire, always a moment to savour. Occasionally some of these

159

outings were with Mum and Dad when they came down to see us, some four or five times in the three years—Mum more than Dad—all they could manage.

The branch line to Looe with its loop from Liskeard and reversal of direction at Coombe Junction under Moorswater Viaduct was my favourite. First, it left Liskeard station at right angles to the main line, going due north, the wrong direction for Looe, curved to the right in a semicircle and dived underneath the main line before continuing to circle back to Moorswater, once more facing north, where the engine changed ends and the train reversed to continue its journey directly south to the sea. The branch line was shaped like a giant question mark with Looe the full stop at the bottom. It went under the main line twice on the circular part. The tiny halts with wooden platforms at St Keyne, Trewidland, Trenant and Duloe, I think were the names, brought us to Sandplace, the tidal limit of the East Looe River. Beside the widening estuary, the train continued past tidal mudflats until the confluence of the East Looe and West Looe Rivers opened out the view. There was a portion of the water on the far side fenced off to make the boating lake on which we would later have an hour if we were lucky. Out at Looe station to walk along the quayside with all sorts of fish in crates for us to examine curiously. They looked nothing like the fish, or bits of them, that we had on our plates to eat. These were surprising, had more detail, often an iridescent beauty, but mostly to our ignorant eyes were far more ugly, more from another planet than merely another familiar element. The

Mum, Jack and me in the Court outside
7 Railway Cottages

lobsters and crabs in baskets had more character, more foreignness when seen here, tentacles and claws waving, sightless eyes staring, still alive, just out of the sea.

Occasionally a Royal Navy motor torpedo boat with a gun on its bow and torpedo tubes with torpedoes lashed on the deck would cruise menacingly in from the sea or be berthed. We longed for a trip in one of those, but never got it. Inspecting them from the quayside, we imagined those tubes unleashing hell at U-boats out in the Channel, though I don't think many were there: they were all in the Atlantic sinking our convoys.

As the river reached the sea it was contained by a high hill to the west and a longish jetty to the east. This jetty ensured that the entrance to the port was navigable. It also helped to create the sandy beach that stretched away eastwards and on which we could play and bathe in specified areas between the tank traps, pill-boxes and barbed wire, there to repel the Germans. There were, reputedly, mined areas too with warning skull-and-crossbones notices, but I don't remember them and I think I would. We spent most time in the rock pools—I once caught in a toy bucket a cuttlefish the size of my hand, to me a weird, alien creature which I wanted to take home but was persuaded to put back. After a day on the beach if it was fine we wandered round the town, looking fruitlessly for an ice cream, having fish (now reassuringly white and flaky) and chips with pop, or tea in a café and—the highlight before we took the train home—an hour on the boating lake, rowing round and incompetently round. I learned the hard way not to have one foot on land and one on the unmoored boat as you board it. I stood there, while Jack rowed fruitlessly to keep the boat where it was, my legs spreading until I was dropped waist-deep into the water in the widening gap.

To get to Polperro we took a bus from Looe. Polperro was Mum's favourite. 'Quaint' was the word I most often heard used to describe it. Now a tourist trap, packed with Cornish ephemera, it was then utterly deserted, bereft of its pre-war trade. Only the port produced income—from the fishing. There was the odd newsagent's which had unsold picture postcards, and I first learned the word 'piskie'—Cornish for 'pixie'—from those cards in Polperro and saw the illustrated prayer that was before the war—and has been since—posted round the world: 'From ghosties and ghoulies and long-leggedy beasties and things that go bump in the night, good Lord deliver us.' Even I, not yet ten, succumbed to the charm of the place as I followed Mum and Dad from one chocolate-box view to another.

Newquay was a much more adventurous journey. Three stops down the main line to St Blazey, then a branch line which had exotic halts called Luxulyan, Bugle, Victoria, Indian Queens and Mount Joy. Unfortunately the landscape we rode through did not match the place names. A large area of undistinguished, low, flattish moorland dotted with vast, melancholy china-clay tips, alternated with the great gashes in the ground from which they had been dug. It always seemed a very dreary place in my mind, though with a bit of sun on it it was probably better.

The little tank engine finally pulled us into

Newquay on the north coast. The railway had made Newquay. Once the line had been opened it had grown from Victorian times into the famous seaside resort that we all knew of, packed all season. It was now deserted in high summer. There was an apocryphal story that circulated the railway community of Doublebois—and no doubt much wider—of the porter on Newquay station who saved all his tips from the pre-war holiday seasons and bought a row of cottages, which he let out during the summer, enjoying a well-heeled retirement on the rents. The story was probably not that apocryphal.

We always made straight for the glorious beaches, unscarred by barbed wire as I remember, perhaps because nobody imagined the Germans would sail round Land's End and attempt a landing there. If the tide was out there was mile upon mile of empty, clean sand with streams to dam. Shrimps and lots of little creatures came out of the sand to greet the wavelets as the tide flowed swiftly in, all preyed on by seabirds and waders and examined by me. Above all there was the surf. We never dared into the big stuff but it was the first time I experienced the fun of standing up to my thighs in freezing water with a foaming wall bearing down on me, to knock me over and carry me back onto the beach spluttering, choking and exhilarated. Shivering to pieces, you towelled yourself down or, better still, had Mum or Auntie Rose do it for you. All in all, Newquay was always the most exciting trip.

Another journey that Auntie Rose took us on, only once, I think, was to Wadebridge and Padstow. We went through a village on the branch

Dad, Jack and me on Newquay beach

line with the glorious name of Washaway.

At Wadebridge the Great Western Railway met the Southern Railway line which came down north of Bodmin Moor from Launceston and Okehampton. It was a measure of our estrangement from home that the green livery of the Southern Railway coaches looked drab after the Great Western chocolate and cream, and the un-Great Western shape of their engines with the numbers painted on instead of on fitted metal number plates looked alien—even inferior—to our eyes. Our own and Dad's Southern Railway a second-class stranger. What next?

Wadebridge, with its arched bridge over the river, I remember only as being gaunt, granite and dull. We trailed after Auntie Rose looking at the uninteresting shops, then onto a Southern Railway train to trundle along the ravishing Camel Estuary to Padstow, another 'quaint' fishing village that tumbled in down the hills on all sides on to the port. The only item of interest to us boys was that the railway line went straight on to the quay to get the fish directly from the boats and then away non-stop to Billingsgate. My principal memory of Padstow is the smell of fish, not unpleasant but very strong.

*　　　*　　　*

Jimmy Peters and I went to Bodmin one day, I think to visit a relative of his in hospital. The hospital was next to the county lunatic asylum, a place of outlandish stories about the mad men and women who inhabited it. We walked across some gardens to the hospital and saw a few pathetic,

166

vacant-looking people shuffling about on the grass. Are they the dangerous lunatics, I wondered. No, I was told later, the dangerous ones are locked away; I believed that, but the sight of those in the gardens stayed with me as the sad image of madness, blotting out the demented screamers of my previous dreams.

We managed to buy a *Beano*, quite an event, and read it together on the train back. One of the comic strips, about Mussolini, the Italian Fascist dictator, was called 'Musso Da Wop, He's A Bigga Da Flop', which we found uncontrollably funny. We were overcome by giggles which we could not contain as we sat in the full compartment. People stared, then smiled and soon were chuckling with us. The better their humour, the more hysterical we got. Perhaps playing to the audience, we speechlessly pointed to the drawings and captions, the reasons for our incontinence. The adults' good humour grew and we all got out to change at Bodmin Road with grins on our faces and said goodbye like old friends. Then the fun evaporated, everything went flat. We stood spaced along the platform waiting for our train, once more back in our own separate worlds. The whole group of us embarrassed, it seemed, by our former exuberance.

*　　　*　　　*

A circus came to Liskeard. The children were told to bring money to school to book a seat if they wanted to go in a party. I was left out. Somehow or other Jack and I failed to ask Auntie Rose for the money. I don't believe she would have refused us.

Or she or Uncle Jack had said circuses were trashy things, or this one would be no good, or Jack was doing something else (what else would a boy be doing when the circus was coming to town?) and I was too shy to ask—another unlikely prospect. Anyway, I was alone, didn't have a ticket and felt very hard done by when most of the children crowded onto the bus and left school early. A few of us remained to scatter drearily to our homes.

'You're early. What's up?' asked Auntie Rose when I got in.

'Everybody's gone to the circus early from school.'

'Well, why haven't you gone?' she said, surprised.

I was near tears when I realised I could have been on that bus. It was all a misunderstanding. Now there was no bus and the next train would be too late. Auntie Rose gave me the entrance money, a shilling and sixpence, plus the fare home from Liskeard in case I couldn't get on the bus coming back, a sandwich, and pushed me out to thumb a lift from one of the rare passing cars or lorries. Actually, I needed no pushing. I ran towards Dobwalls. I ran through Dobwalls, still no cars. Out of Dobwalls, down the winding hill and up the long, long drag past Moorswater. Still no lift. Four miles I covered and arrived at the circus, pitched in a field between Liskeard station and the town, to find that the show had started and, anyway, the marquee was full. I stood there with no breath, gasping with exhaustion and frustration, only just holding down my sobs.

My heartbeats and breathing slowed down as I wandered about listening to the laughter and

168

applause from inside, more gall to my soul. Someone was selling candyfloss, unheard of during the war. It tasted filthy even to my eager tongue. I couldn't finish it. I went round the back and saw some dejected-looking ponies, which I tried to pat until abruptly told to leave them alone. I moved resentfully away among the circus people who were bustling about.

Just as I was about to give up, a baby elephant came out of the marquee, having done its stuff for the moment. This creature, with its huge ears and searching active trunk, seemed like a miracle. I swear it glowed. It stood shorter than I did and must have been very young. I stared at it in wonder, then sidled up to it and was allowed to pat it. I felt the sensitive top of its trunk explore my clothes, searching for my sandwich, I suppose. This was no mirage but a wonderfully solid, magical, gigantic pet. I asked its handler, an unbossy woman, if I could give him some sandwich. She inspected it and said yes, adding, 'She's not a him.' So, breaking my sandwich into the smallest pieces I could, I fed it bit by bit to the elephant, who stood there waiting for more, its trunk running over my clothes and hands, thrilling me with its touch, not always gentle, always demanding. When my sandwich was finished I asked the woman what else the elephant liked.

'Fruit,' she said.

'What fruit?'

'Apples.'

I raced out of the field to the nearest greengrocer's, still just open, bought a pound of apples and tore back. The elephant was gone. Lungs again bursting I nearly cried with frustration but it reappeared from the tent, having done another turn. It headed straight for me; I nearly died with joy—elephants, apparently, do remember—and I fed it the apples until told by the woman that that was enough, she had to take her away. I patted my new best friend goodbye, tried and failed to hold her trunk for a moment, watched her amble away, spent my remaining pennies on a bag of chips, had my last apple and, penniless, walked contentedly home.

CHAPTER FOURTEEN

Uncle Jack's antipathy to all things religious turned a minor incident involving Miss Polmanor into a comic and shaming episode. It was their polarised attitudes that caused it and I am certain that he, at least, regretted it. His atheism was founded on or confirmed by his experiences in the First World War. Any faith he may have had was—like the faith of many others—blown to pieces in the trenches along with the thousands of their comrades and nominal enemies. His real enemies were not German soldiers, of course, but all people with civilian power over him: bosses, owners, all officers above a certain rank, staff officers perhaps, who ordered the soldiers into danger as opposed to sharing it with them. Bestriding all of his world was religious authority, then so much more important than now. So a woman like Miss Polmanor, who, though she paraded her faith, was in reality a sad lonely figure (as Auntie Rose recognised), was a red rag.

Some Saturdays Uncle Jack would take Jack and me into Dobwalls for our regular visit to the barber. There, in a glass-covered annex to a house on the right just as we entered the village, sat a barber's chair which looked across the road at Rowe's garage opposite and at Ede's village shop on its right. A smaller road and three lanes joined the main road here; it was as near to a focal point that a village which straggled along one road for over half a mile could have. The house was a few steps above street-level so the barber's chair was a splendid place from which to watch the world—or Dobwalls, anyway—go by. And to gossip. Uncle Jack sat there chatting to the barber while his little ring of hair was cut even shorter and shaved at the neck. Jack and I—and all the other children in the village—were seated on a board set across the arms of the chair and ruthlessly given pudding-basin haircuts in spite of our wriggles. Up the back of the neck and over the crown went the clippers, short back and sides it was called, very nearly short back, sides and top. This haircut was thought to keep the nits to a minimum and it probably did. A forelock was all that was left of my former fair-haired tangle; my mother hated it when she visited: her boys in hobnail boots and cropped hair like hobbledehoys.

One Saturday, with newly shorn heads and itchy bits of hair caught down the inside of our shirts, we left the barber's to see if there were any sweets or comics to be bought in Ede's. It was a busy morning: there were several vackies and village kids in the road, some villagers were chatting and Miss Polmanor arrived on her bicycle with its shopping basket.

In the shop children were pestering Mr Ede. 'Haven't you got the *Beano*?' 'No *Dandy*?' 'Any gobstoppers?' 'No sweets at all?'

He was a pleasant man who got on with most people. 'No, no, no, us don't have naught.'

'You said you'd have the *Beano* today.'

'Us can't do naught about the paper shortage.'

'You've got the *Farmers Weekly*.'

'That's vital for the war effort.'

And the children would make a ragged chorus of that ritual answer to all complaints: 'Oh yeah. There's a war on.'

'Go on, you children, off you go. Don't block up the shop. What can I do for you, Miss Polmanor?'

She was rummaging anxiously. 'I've got my list here but I can't find my purse.'

Mr Ede addressed Uncle Jack. 'Morning, Mr Phillips, what can I do for you?'

Before Uncle Jack could answer, Miss Polmanor spoke loudly. She was getting agitated. 'My money. 'Tis not yere. I must have been robbed.'

'Perhaps you dropped it,' said Mr Ede helpfully.

'No, I can't have.' She gestured to demonstrate. ' 'Twas in my purse, which was in my handbag, which was in my shopping bag, which was in my basket.'

Uncle Jack couldn't resist such an opening. He chipped in with a friendly smile. 'Must have been Dick Turpin to get that off you.'

Miss Polmanor's temperature went up. ' 'Tis not funny, Mr Phillips.'

'Did you leave it in the off-licence?' His concerned expression looked quite real.

'How dare you!' She was quite rattled by this and went too far. 'They children jostled I just now.

172

One o' they must have taken it.'

Uncle Jack took this seriously. He rounded on us. 'Have one of you got Miss Polmanor's purse?'

Fervent denials all round.

'There.' He spread his hands to her as though the matter were concluded.

Mr Ede was genuinely helpful. 'Look round on the floor, my dear. 'Er must be yere somewhere.'

Everyone started looking.

'There's more than two pounds in there,' wailed Miss Polmanor.

We all redoubled our efforts, some of the children overdoing it a bit. 'Wow.' 'Quick. Where is it?' 'Do I get a reward?'

A vackie called John White started to leave the shop. Miss Polmanor jumped on him. 'Where be you going?'

'I was gonna look outside,' said John, upset at the implications.

'Escaping, were you?' She went on to dig her own grave, something she had probably done her whole life. 'You'm hiding it somewhere.'

John, a gentle boy who later became a Methodist minister, was near tears. 'I haven't got your rotten purse.'

'Us should search all of 'em. One of 'em has it, 'tis sure,' continued the distracted Miss Polmanor.

Uncle Jack strolled to the door, seething. He muttered, 'I don't think I can stand it in yere.' He raised his voice. 'I suppose I can leave, can I? Without being searched?' and added to me, 'I'll be outside, boy, when you're released.' He growled something in Welsh as he left.

Miss Polmanor pointed at me, perhaps someone she felt she could trust. 'You stand guard by the

173

door, boy.'

Once more I was her unwilling accomplice.

Mr Ede, too, was upset. 'Well, how's us gwain to search they?'

She was at a loss for only a moment. 'The boys can empty they'm pockets to start with.'

The boys reluctantly started to do this as, outside, I saw Uncle Jack meet Jack, who had been talking to a friend. 'Look, Uncle Jack, I've just found this purse over by Miss Polmanor's bike.'

Uncle Jack gave a thin, bitter laugh. 'Take it in the shop. She's in there having kittens. Tell her where you found it.'

Inside, the melodrama continued. I had no chance to open my mouth. Mr Ede looked at the girls in their flimsy summer dresses. 'How's us gwain to search they maids? They bain't got nowhere to hide naught.'

One boy pointed at Elsie. 'You'll have to look in her knickers. She puts everything in there.'

Elsie coloured up as all the children except me giggled. To have searched her would have been ludicrous: she lived with Miss Polmanor.

At which moment Jack came in. 'Is this your purse, Miss Polmanor?'

She grabbed it triumphantly. 'There. One of 'em has it. I told you.'

Mr Ede protested that Jack had just come in.

Jack said, 'I found it on the ground by your bicycle.'

Miss Polmanor was humiliated and confused. To cover her embarrassment she checked the contents as Jack added earnestly, 'I didn't look inside, Miss Polmanor. I didn't like to.'

She left, trying to gather the shreds of her

174

dignity. The moment she was outside excited giggles and chatter burst out among the children. 'She blames us for everything.'

'Blinking old bat.'

Mr Ede wasn't having that in his shop and we were all driven out to where Uncle Jack was in conversation with Miss Polmanor. He was chewing a matchstick and grinning. 'So the vackies didn't steal your purse after all, then?'

'Little devils. You don't know what they'll get up to next.' She turned quickly away to her bicycle. 'Oh. Look at this. I've got a puncture. A flat tyre.'

'Oh, bad luck,' said Uncle Jack. Then an even bigger exclamation of sympathy. He pointed at her back wheel. 'Look at that. Both of 'em. That's terrible. Where have you been riding it? In the quarry?'

Miss Polmanor stared at her bike. '*Two* flat tyres. It's they vackies again.'

'But they was all in the shop with you,' said Uncle Jack. 'You kept 'em in there. Remember?'

She was silenced.

He looked away down the road to Doublebois and the army camp. 'I reckon it was one of those two soldiers who were here just now. I saw them fiddling about by your bike.'

Miss Polmanor was near tears. 'Soldiers. Vackies. I've left my pump at home. I'll have to push it all the way.'

Uncle Jack dived to her rescue. I think he was starting to feel genuinely sorry for her. He called the biggest vacky boy over. 'Hey, Frank, wheel Miss Polmanor's bike over to the garage and pump her tyres up for her and she'll give you sixpence.'

She grabbed the bike. 'Don't worry. I can do it

175

myself.'

'No, no, you mustn't. There's help here aplenty.' He turned to Frank again. 'You do it and *I'll* give you sixpence. We can't leave her to do it on her own, can we?' He reached into his pocket. 'Miss Polmanor will just say, "Thank you very much. You're a good boy."'

'I shall do no such thing,' she said firmly and pushed her bike away, leaving everyone longing to say something but waiting till she was out of earshot.

'Cor,' whispered Elsie. 'How did she get two punctures?'

'I reckon someone let her tyres down,' said Frank.

There was much *sotto voce* excitement at this, quite a daring crime in all the circumstances.

'I told her. I think it was those two soldiers. I saw them messing about.' Uncle Jack again pointed vaguely towards Doublebois. 'D'you know how they did it?'

'Easy,' boasted Frank. 'You can do it with a matchstick.'

Uncle Jack took the matchstick from his mouth and gestured with it. 'That's right, boy. You just use the matchstick to push the valve in and . . . psssss . . . there you are.' He gave the matchstick to Frank. 'But don't you ever try it on my bike or I'll tan the hide off you.' He winked at Jack and me. 'Come on, boys. Home for some dinner, is it?'

*　　　*　　　*

Doublebois and Dobwalls were due for more shocks. Once more the soldiers piled into their

Bedford lorries with their kitbags and rifles and rode away, waving to us kids and singing bawdy songs. We again had the run of our glorious playground, Doublebois House and grounds and the empty Nissen huts.

The district just had time to heave a corporate sigh of relief before the rumours started as to who would be next to occupy it. The Land Army? People who had been bombed out? The Commandos? Everyone except the Germans, it seemed. The roar of different motors was soon heard. Vast, high-bonneted, high-sided lorries which the occupants called trucks, with names like Dodge and Chrysler. And jeeps, a stylish updating of the English Land-Rovers. Yes, it was the Americans.

A year earlier Hitler had declared war on them to show solidarity with his friends the Japanese after they attacked Pearl Harbor. Churchill had been trying to get the Americans in from the beginning and Hitler generously did his work for him. The outcome was no longer in any serious doubt. Now England was being flooded with American soldiers prior to D-Day and the invasion of Europe.

In our part of Cornwall, people from the next village were strangers; Englishmen from across the Tamar were foreigners; Americans might have been from Mars. And that wasn't all: to cap everything, they weren't just Americans, they were black, a whole regiment of them. Many in the village had never seen a black man; I don't think I had.

'They'm BLACK,' some squawked at each other.

'What? All over? All the way up and down?'

'They got white palms to their hands, I saw when I shook 'ands wi' one o' they.'

'It wears off, that's why.'

'Does it wash off?'

'They can see in the dark.'

'They'd have to, wouldn't they.'

'And their lips!'

The men lowered their voices. 'They got John Thomases like Crago's bull.'

'Twenty-two inches of uncontrolled flesh.'

'They'm mad for white women,' one man whispered to Miss Polmanor.

She needed no encouragement. 'Us'll all be raped in our beds.'

Her informant reassured her. 'Don't you worry. They'll make an exception in your case.'

It's no good thinking in terms of colour prejudice. The village wasn't prejudiced—it was astounded. Although we were at the centre of the British Empire, populated with millions of every size, shape and colour, this was a remote part of Cornwall in 1943.

And we kids in Doublebois, we loved them. They made our own soldiers seem drab. Their uniforms, their equipment, their cigarettes, their sweets and, above all, their very colour. We wore their hats, chewed their gum, held their strange hands and ate their candy. Rides on army vehicles doubled. Jeeps were the big treat: tooth-loosening, rebounding joy-rides across the fields. We drilled with their rifles and learned their slang. I had a tap-dancing lesson on a sheet of plywood at the army camp gates from a man from New Orleans itself.

I was in Ede's shop with some other people just after they arrived, when a couple of them strolled in. They politely took their caps off and greeted us.

Mr Ede was always kindly but perhaps he sensed trade. He practically curtsied behind the counter. 'You'm welcome to Cornwall. 'Taint much but 'tis home to us.'

'This is paradise. You should see where we come from.' The deep voice and Southern accent astonished me. It wasn't like the voices in the Westerns we had seen every Saturday morning before the war.

A man asked the question all Americans got asked. 'Where you been to these last three years? 'Tis nearly all over.' But it was lost on these two and somehow seemed scarcely fair. All of our images of America were white—with blacks occasionally being goofy or loyal in the background.

The second GI asked, 'Excuse me, ma'am, but we see you have two churches in your city. Is one— maybe—all right for coloured folk to worship in?'

'They be Church of England and Wesleyan Methodist. Which be you?'

'We're Baptist.'

'I reckon that's the same as Methodist, don't you, Miss Polmanor?' someone asked maliciously.

There was another camp concert given with the ubiquitous Looe Fishermen's Choir performing and us kids singing traditional and patriotic songs for our guests. Then their own jazz band played for us. It was sensational; the whole room was soon rocking. I had never heard music like it. But when GIs started jitterbugging there and then in the aisles with each other and the few girls who

179

were present—their dresses swirling up above their waists—it went too far for most. Opinion about our guests' behaviour divided between those who couldn't wait to join in—mostly girls—some who didn't mind, and most—or possibly the most vocal—who were shocked rigid. The arguments to support the shocked-rigid view became wider and wilder. A dance at the army camp, always an attraction for the younger females in entertainment-free Doublebois, Dobwalls and wider, became a must for all who could or dared.

And these smiling, flamboyant-to-us, gentle men who came from God knows what hells in the Deep South of the segregated USA let us pat and pull their hair, rub their skin to see if it came off, examine their pink palms, marvel at their very existence—and then they were gone just as suddenly as they had appeared and were replaced by other Yanks, white ones, no less friendly, no less generous, but with not a tenth of the exotic appeal of their black comrades.

CHAPTER FIFTEEN

Fighting was a part of living for a boy, most boys I suppose, in those days. I know that I was always willing to defend myself or my position or my rights even if the other boy was a bit bigger. And not just to defend myself. I was willing to attack, too. If he was too big I would hit him and run. I don't think I was brave; we just thought like that. It established pecking orders and settled disputes, even for boys as young as me. At first the vackies fought the village kids. When that calmed down and many vackies had returned home—quite a few simply became fourteen, left school and went home to work—so that we were outnumbered, we fought each other, God knows what about. I remember having a strolling casual fight with Alan Packham all the way home from school one day while his older brother Harold walked with us and looked on. We were evenly matched in age and size; we walked a bit, punched a bit, walked and skirmished, breathing heavily from emotion as much as exertion; it was inconclusive. When he reached his house, the district nurse's house across the road, he went in and I walked the few yards to the Court. I crept into the wash-house, washed the blood off and bathed the scratches from where we had fallen into the hedge as we grappled, before going in for my tea. Such things can't have been as casual as all that, feelings and passions were clearly involved, but that is how I remember them, the causes long forgotten.

There was one fight, though, that was serious and stays in my memory. I was just ten, we had been in Cornwall for nearly three years and had just been given our end-of-term reports for Easter term 1943. By this time in the war the bombing seemed to be over so most of the vackies had already gone home (though we still had the V1 and V2 raids to come). We few who were left had been incorporated into the village school. I was top of my class and, indeed, the whole school, which had pupils up to the age of fourteen. This was no great academic achievement, the bright kids over eleven were already creamed off to Liskeard County School, and the child who came second to me was an eight-year-old Jewish boy in my class called Goodman, a recently bombed-out vacky from another part of London. He was, unlike me, a genuinely clever boy, two years younger, breathing down my neck and looking as though he would soon pass me. Jack, having reached fourteen, was going to go back home to Woolwich Polytechnic to extend his education. I was soon to sit the entrance exam for grammar school, an event dreaded by most, but not by me. Coming top must have made me insufferable, certainly to my brother. I don't remember precisely what happened but perhaps I crowed once too often, perhaps a teacher said something to Jack about me being an example to him—as though he hadn't had enough of that all of his life. Perhaps a combination of the two. It could even be that I was less guilty for the fracas than I still feel about it and Jack was less generous than I am painting him.

Anyway, he who had shown a whole childhood's forbearance to his uppity young brother, hit me on the way home from school. This was a huge shock. I was surprised and hurt, not necessarily physically, and I furiously ran at him to hit him back. He defended himself easily and we had a long trail back to Doublebois, walking apart, punctuated with futile rushes from me and flung insults—I was good at those—between bitter sobs and recriminations. The other children kept well ahead, walking briskly on and staying out of this family squabble.

At home Auntie Rose quickly got to the bottom of who we had been fighting: each other. She was shocked. 'You hit your little brother?' she demanded of Jack in a voice that frightened us both and had him in tears of guilt and shame. I was sent out to the wash-house to clean myself up and put cold water—as though there was any other sort to wash in—on the back of my neck to stop the nosebleed. She was closeted with Jack and the two reports. I listened outside the window.

To my surprise I heard Jack receive no telling off for hitting me—though he cried from time to time and I could hear the indrawn sobs as he tried to stop himself. Instead, Auntie Rose paid him strings of compliments about how he had taken on the responsibility of me when we were originally evacuated, how he had looked after me, what a good boy he was, how he was always helpful and hard-working, utterly trustworthy, how he looked after his allotment and produced food for us all, how much she admired him because he was so like Uncle Jack, who had looked after her and their children through the awful time of the Great Depression. And, biggest surprise of all, how clever he was. Not just book-and-sums clever like me, but really clever and Wise about Life. When he was back in London and at the Poly he would soon overtake me and then we would all see. She called me in and sent me on an errand.

When I returned Uncle Jack had arrived home from work. He and Auntie Rose were closeted together briefly. He went out to the wash-house. Still in neutral gear with me she handed me my report and told me to take it out to him. 'There,' she said. 'Surprise him. See what he thinks about that.' Auntie Rose, impressed by learning, was normally very pleased by my reports, so I was fooled.

No matter what my report and the teachers said I was clearly pretty slow in some departments because, as I took it to him, pride reasserted itself; I was expecting more praise. 'I've got my report, Uncle Jack.'

'Oh yes?' he said non-committally.

'From school.'

'From school? That's unusual. Fancy, your report comes from school. Get me a bowl of water from the tap, there's a lad. I'll wash some of this muck off.'

I couldn't go fast enough. But Uncle Jack stripped off his jacket and hung it up, then his waistcoat, carefully rolled up his sleeves, sluiced his arms, hands, face and shining bald head. He dried off, took me into the house, removed his boots, put on his glasses and sat in the armchair to read the golden report.

I was bursting. 'I got all nines and tens. I only lost five marks in the whole exam. Every subject.'

'Five marks?' He was sharp. 'Five? What d'you lose them for?'

I gaped at the question, breathless. My world turned upside down. It's not what you achieve, but how far you fall short that matters. 'Er—well—um—well—I—er—two were silly mistakes, I really knew the answers, and three were taken off for untidiness.'

'Carelessness, is it? I'm bringing up carelessness yere, am I? That won't do, will it, boy? Let's see all tens next time.'

'But I came top of the whole school. Some of them are nearly fifteen.'

Uncle Jack was contemptuous. 'Bloody yokels. Clods. Cockneys and farm labourers. What do they

184

know? Tens, boy, next time. Tens. And less of this untidiness. And remember: when you're top dog no one likes a clever Dick. That often results in losing friends, the ones you might call thick. And if you think I'm being hard, well, life's never bloody fair. Pass me the newspaper.'

We had our tea. The meal seemed to be finished and only Jack and I sat, still subdued, at the table. Auntie Rose put a bowl in front of each of us. 'Yere you are, your favourite: blackberry-and-apple pie, over from Sunday. But I'm not sure you deserve it.'

She left us to get on with what we thought was the best pudding ever. I had an idea. 'I'm not hungry, Jack. Would you like mine?'

He stared at me and at my plate, aware that there was more to this offer than pie, but not sure what. 'D'you mean that?'

'Yes. Honest.'

'OK.' Somewhere round about then the penny must have dropped. 'No. I'll tell you what: I'll have half.'

'OK.'

I carefully cut mine into halves and spooned one of them onto his plate, watched by him. He looked at my plate, then at his full one. 'There's too much there. I can't eat all of that. Would you like half of mine?'

'All right.'

Jack measured and cut his portion, picked up his plate and carefully spooned half of his pie onto my plate till both were equally charged. 'That's fair, isn't it?'

I nodded.

We ate our blackberry-and-apple pie in the

peace brokered by Auntie Rose and Uncle Jack.

*　　　*　　　*

Jack and I were doing our homework after school one evening. Auntie Rose was listening to something on the radio so we were banished to the front room instead of the cosiness of the kitchen table in the middle of the life of the house. This was unusual so we went grumpily. Uncle Jack came in from work. The radio was turned up but we easily heard why we had been sent out. She said, quite quietly, 'Elsie's pregnant.'

'There's a surprise,' said Uncle Jack, showing none whatsoever.

'Three months gone.'

'Who knows?'

'Miss Polmanor, for one.'

'Everybody, then.'

There was a silence broken only by the radio as Jack and I breathlessly listened. Auntie Rose broke it. 'I wonder if she knows who the father is.'

Uncle Jack's footsteps were taking him to the back door and the wash-house. They stopped. 'If you eat a tin of baked beans how do you know which one made you fart?' And his steps receded before she could answer.

*　　　*　　　*

I found Elsie down the gardens beyond the outside privies, somewhere she didn't usually go. She was crying. This upset me terribly, no childhood outbreak of tears but something grown-up and important. 'Elsie, Elsie, don't cry. I love you.'

186

'Oh, shut up,' she sobbed.

'I'll stay here with you.'

'Bugger off.' I didn't move. 'Go on, bugger off. Leave me alone.'

I ran back to the house. 'Auntie Rose, Auntie Rose.'

'Calm down, boy. What's up?'

'Elsie's crying,' was all I could think of saying.

'She'll do a lot more of that.'

'Have I got to marry her?' I blurted out.

At last Auntie Rose reacted in a way that matched the situation. 'What?' She stared at me.

'I'm the father.'

She laughed, an entirely unexpected event. 'Don't be silly, boy.'

'But I am. I—' I struggled to express what we had done. What had we done? I wasn't at all sure. 'I—I kissed her.'

I was dismissed. 'If you've finished your homework you can go out and play. Go on.'

I started to cry, not at all sure why. 'But I love her. She said she loves me.'

'It's not what she said to you that matters. It's what she did with someone else. Go on. Out.'

*   *   *

Elsie and I met frequently in spite of her telling me to bugger off. I was someone she could share things with, after all. Life must have been a bleak business living with Miss Polmanor. I have no idea what Auntie Rose's views were, moral or practical, on the subject of unmarried pregnancies—and I cannot believe she condoned them—but her natural compassion asserted itself. Elsie was a girl she was fond of who needed help. That was that. Uncle Jack, equally kind, would always go along with his wife in such matters, anyway. So Elsie was an even more frequent visitor to 7 Railway Cottages. The rest of Doublebois more or less accepted it: 'There's a war on.' Pregnant girls were becoming more numerous everywhere—especially since the Yanks had arrived. Although on that score there were those who thought girls who went with Yanks were not only tarts but also traitors to 'Our Boys'.

When everyone else was out, Elsie and I giggled over her rounded tummy. 'That's the baby. D'you remember when you didn't believe me about babies?'

'I was young then.'

'Feel it. It moves.'

I did and was startled, repulsed, I think. 'Erggh. 'Slike a frog squirming.'

'I hope 'er's a Yank. They was best,' was a remark she often made to my shocked ears.

I hadn't seen her for a while when I saw her walking down the road from Dobwalls. I ran to meet her and laughed with shocked surprise. 'Cor, Elsie, your stomach's enormous.'

She was in no mood for childish pleasantries. Her face was set. Her mood angry. 'They're going to send me away.'

I was stopped in my tracks. 'Oh no.'

'To a home, they said. Where I'll be looked after, they said.'

I was desperate. 'I'll look after you, Elsie. I love you.'

She ignored me, looking into her own hell. 'This home'll be full of girls what have had babies from

188

soldiers. They'll all be adopted. We'm "fallen women", somebody said in the village.'

'We can go to our hut in the woods, Elsie. We can live there together.'

'Don't be simple,' and she strode furiously away to Miss Polmanor's, leaving me shattered in the road.

CHAPTER SIXTEEN

Singing became part of my life in Cornwall. It seems that I sang all the time. We sang at school in assembly and in music classes: a hymn in assembly and all the well-known folk songs and children's songs in class, plus the occasional more serious piece. We played singing games in school breaks; as I have said, the vackies and village kids even sang our antagonism at each other, and when that was over we sang children's chants, games and popular songs together. At home the Light Programme was always on the radio with Auntie Rose joining in through the day and encouraging us to do the same: 'Come on, boys, I sound like a crow. You can do better than that.' So we sang not only the current hits but songs from previous years back to Victorian ballads and the music hall. We sang in church on Sundays and carols at Christmas.

I said at the beginning of this story how our mother introduced us to the Russians, the Romantics, Ravel, Debussy, serious twentieth-century music starting with Stravinsky and lots of popular music and jazz, which she played to us and for her own pleasure. Well, Uncle Jack introduced us to a different range. There were the Welsh songs that he loved and the folk songs and children's songs that we knew from school, but the surprise was that atheist Uncle Jack showed us the beauty and majesty of the harmonies in *Hymns Ancient and Modern* and other ecclesiastical choral music. He never objected to our attending church on a Sunday—not that he would have dared cross Auntie Rose on the subject—indeed, he often came himself, turning the old 'Why should the Devil have all the best tunes?' into 'Why should God have all the best music? He's not listening anyway, so we might as well.'

Jack like me was a member of the choir at St Peter's church. But when he reached fourteen, voice wavering between alto and croak, he preferred to have his turn on a Sunday, like all the older boys, pumping the organ for sixpence; I was never big enough. All sorts of (really rather mild) naughtinesses were indulged in by those on duty, out of sight behind the organ between hymns; their whispers and stifled giggles were given black looks by the vicar and others. Occasionally it would get out of hand when the boys did not pay attention to the service and forgot the few pumps necessary to get the organ primed. The organist would touch the keys and, instead of the opening chord, the instrument would let out a dying, groaning sigh that made you have to struggle not to let out a snort of laughter into the solemn Sunday silence. Some boy would be given the dreadful punishment of being forbidden to pump and having to sit in the congregation each week with no sixpence. Although I regretted not being a part of the bigger-boy fraternity that actually got paid for doing such a desirable job, I loved being in the choir above all else. A few years later back in Welling I remember how sad I was when my voice broke. I certainly never embraced puberty.

I have long since been an atheist myself but I remain grateful and glad that I have a Church of England background. It gave me so much, not only musically but also with regard to the English language, architecture and other cultural spin-offs. I doubt if I would feel the same if I had met it a century or more earlier, when it still held real sway over people's minds and lives, but I seem to have met it at just the right moment in its decline. In spite of all the sexual inhibitions and guilt that it left me with I remain indebted to my Church of England background that has brought me so many unexpected riches. Our national religion was all around us in those days, at school, in our language, on the wireless, in our national consciousness, in a way that it is no longer. It gave us boundaries and shape to our view of the world and it was Auntie Rose who set us on the road by insisting that we went to church and Sunday school, and Uncle Jack who made us listen to the beauty, both musical and verbal. I still use for reference, or just to read the language, my King James Bible and *The Book of Common Prayer* presented to me in September 1940 and September 1942 for Sunday-school attendance and inscribed by the shadowy Reverend Oatey. Unfortunately I have lost my *Hymns Ancient and Modern*, which probably has 'September 1941' written inside it. The best of religions, full of glory and utterly ineffectual.

I used to go and play often with the Burfords, Pat, June, Peter and Derek, at Treburgie Farm,

191

near East Taphouse, where they lived. An avenue of magnificent beech trees led to the farm. As soon as I reached it I would start to sing. This avenue formed a natural nave which sent my voice echoing back to me. Alone in my beautiful cathedral I used to let rip with all my being into whatever we were rehearsing at the time and into my favourites. 'Jerusalem', of course, was one of them and I would send it soaring up into the branches to come back at me. My voice never sounded better and it gave me the confidence to stand up and sing it in the East Cornwall Silver Voice competition one anti-acoustic day in Liskeard cattle market when sound was shredded by lowing cattle, bleating sheep and a gusting wind. The marketers stood in respectful silence while we children entertained them but it must have been thin gruel. I won, possibly because I was the loudest, and was presented with a half-crown's worth of National Savings stamps and a bucketful of pride for Auntie Rose and Uncle Jack.

One Christmas towards the end of my time there Betty Cormack and I sang the carol 'Good King Wenceslas' in costume to the school, indeed the whole village. She was the King and I was his/her page. Auntie Rose sat beaming at me from the audience and Uncle Jack looked suitably critical. The downside of that was that I had to write about it in detail to Mum and Dad. Well, at least I had a subject for my letter that week.

Cornwall is probably the warmest county in the country but when the wind swung round the wrong way and came down off the moor it used to cut through us as we walked to school and back; we would run home to get out of it. One Christmas had a brief, very cold snap. There was more than a smattering of snow on the ground being blown into your face by a biting northerly wind. Under the snow were sheets of ice, which had fallen as rain and froze before the snow came. By Boxing Night we children must have been driving our parents and foster-parents mad because we were all let out, or perhaps sent out, to play. The Plummers, Jack and me huddled in the Court. We hit on the idea of going carol singing, unusual, as far as I remember, in our world. We collected Jimmy Peters, the Bunney children, Harold and Alan Packham. Eight or ten of us gathered. Someone found an old tin and we punched a slot into the lid. We had our collecting box. We wrote 'Mrs Churchill's Russian Red Cross' on the side of the tin, so it must have been 1941 or more likely '42, by which time the Russians had been invaded by the Germans and were on our side. We started singing in the Court, were given some money and set off into the blackest of nights. We didn't notice the temperature or wind-chill in our enthusiasm. Half a mile up the road to Dobwalls were some cottages down a lane. We sang and knocked, were given some money, sang some more and went on our way. Down the road to Crago's farm. The same story. Across another half-mile of frozen field to the houses on the Lostwithiel road, where some sort of party was in progress. We were asked into the glorious warmth and stood in rows, singing the parts, solos and in unison to the householders and their guests, who smiled benevolently at us as we performed. They applauded us, gave us food, drink and money, and off we went. Another trek across fields and down lanes. More coins clanking into our tin. We stopped at a crossroads, crouched in a circle and emptied it on to the icy tarmac to count it by the light of a torch. On through the bitter dark night with tingling fingers, ears and toes to other isolated houses and finally triumphantly home. Fifteen shillings, we raised. We got a postal order, sent it off and proudly showed everyone our letter of acknowledgement signed by Mrs Churchill herself.

CHAPTER SEVENTEEN

Some sort of a Silver Voice competition was held every year in many villages. Jack and I were to sing a duet, coached by Uncle Jack: 'Sheep May Safely Graze' by Johann Sebastian, Jack singing the alto line, me the treble. Uncle Jack wanted us to win this for many reasons: his Welsh pride in singing; his previous work with Gwyn; his desire to beat the 'God-botherers' in their own backyard. It must have been in 1943 because Jack was due to go back to London to the Poly and Elsie was heavily pregnant. The competition was to be held in Dobwalls Methodist Chapel, the largest space in the village—someone had realised that the cattle market was no place for children's voices. Jack kept complaining to Uncle Jack that his voice was 'going funny'.

'Don't you dare let it break till after the competition,' Uncle Jack said.

We arrived at the Methodist chapel along with most of the district. I had tried to persuade Elsie to come but she had refused; she was too shy or ashamed to go to such a gathering with her burgeoning stomach and, had she asked, I am sure Miss Polmanor would have refused permission for her even to leave the house in such shape: literally publicising her sin. We all sat in a state of excitement as the chapel filled. Auntie Rose pulled my sock up, straightened Jack's tie, ineffectually smoothed our cropped hair. 'There. You look a pair now, both of you.' Her favourite compliment.

'Nervous, boys?' asked Uncle Jack.

'A bit.'

'That's good. You should be. Take good big breaths, you'll see 'em all off.'

The congregation sang 'Ye Holy Angels Bright' with its glorious descant and all the competitors' voices were warmed up.

The Reverend Clifford Buckroyd welcomed us all while the Reverend R. O. Oatey sat beside him and smiled vaguely: joint denominational events were rare. Buckroyd led us in a prayer which beseeched God to give the children tuneful voices and the judges clear minds. Like all prayers of whatever denomination it finished with ' . . . and bless all our forces, army, navy and air force, wherever they may be', always followed by a fervent 'Amen' from everyone.

During the prayer, while everyone's head was lowered, someone slipped onto the bench beside me, nudging me along. It was Elsie. She grinned covertly, proud of her own daring. I was both glad and embarrassed to see her there.

Uncle Jack had no such qualms. 'Hello, Elsie,' he said, none too quietly. 'You decided to support us, then, is it?'

Elsie grinned briefly as I was aware of something else going on. Miss Polmanor was on her feet. 'Mr Buckroyd. Mr Buckroyd.'

'Yes, Miss Polmanor?'

'In view of the fact that most of the children of the village are here this evening, I wonder if you fully approve of the congregation?'

What on earth was this? Some sort of attack on the fact that C of E people were in her Wesleyan chapel?

Buckroyd was equally confused. 'I don't think I quite understand, Miss Polmanor.'

'This is a children's occasion. We should be protecting them. From corruption. From lewdness.'

The penny was dropping all round the chapel. There were murmurs and a muttered 'Hear, hear'.

Elsie squirmed beside me. 'Oh, no. Oh, no.'

I must say, no matter what I thought of Miss Polmanor, she had guts, the conviction of her beliefs. She had already reported Elsie to the authorities, sparking off the decision to have her sent away to a home, but she hadn't kicked her out, that would have been unchristian. But now she was prepared to stand up in public and make a fuss about Elsie attending this gathering when she should have been invisible at home. 'While our menfolk are away fighting God's holy war we womenfolk should be setting an example, not pointing the way down the primrose path to damnation. I think you all know to whom I refer.' She didn't even need to point at Elsie.

There were more murmurs, a louder 'Hear, hear', and Elsie got to her feet. Whatever battles Elsie had fought and won against Miss Polmanor when they were at home, she was thoroughly cowed now.

'I'm sorry, Mr Buckroyd. I am, honest. I only came to hear the boys sing. I'll go—I—'

A hand came across me and grabbed her. 'You bloody sit down and don't move,' growled Uncle Jack. It was the showdown he must have been dreaming of for twenty years since the 1918 armistice.

Elsie was crying. 'No, no, I—'

Everything started to go very fast. People were talking loudly as Miss Polmanor said, 'I saw her. She slipped in while we were all at prayer', as Buckroyd said, 'Please, Miss Polmanor, I am sure there is no need—' and Uncle Jack topped it all with, 'What's she supposed to have done then, eh, missus?'

Auntie Rose pulled at Uncle Jack's sleeve without much conviction. 'Oh Jack, don't make a scene,' but I am sure she was on his side; it was only her natural aversion to public display that prompted her to object.

Miss Polmanor's voice rose above the hubbub. 'Sinned. As well you know, Mr Phillips. Sinned again and again.' Three years of failure with Elsie's morals tinged her voice.

Buckroyd managed to get in with 'Please, please, this is a house of God.'

'Durst we not mention sin in the house of God now?'

'Elsie may have transgressed—' began Buckroyd.

Uncle Jack had the best pair of lungs there. He used them now. 'Let him or *her* that is without sin cast the first stone.'

197

'I was about to use those very words,' said Buckroyd.

'Then what's all this transgressing?' said Uncle Jack. 'She did what come natural.'

'I intended no censure,' said Buckroyd.

'Then why *not*?' Miss Polmanor was indignant.

Poor Buckroyd, under attack from two directions. Oatey, as far as I remember, wisely stayed out of it all. The place was seething by now, with people taking sides, joining in or just sitting, fascinated by some entertainment they had never expected, much better than children warbling.

Uncle Jack continued without pause. 'And if anyone should leave this house, you should order *her* out . . .'

Mr Buckroyd chimed in, 'Mr Phillips, I'm not ordering anyone out. That's not my—'

'. . . for the sin of envy. We all know she'd like to have been in this state years ago only no one'd touch her, bloody dried-up old haybag.'

We were all shocked at this. It took the row into another dimension.

Buckroyd showed his dismay. 'Oh, now, Mr Phillips, that is not Christian.'

'Well, I'm not one of them, thank God. Come on, Rose. Come on, boys, let's breathe some clear air outside. Elsie, you want to walk home with us, is it?'

*   *   *

As far as I know East Cornwall never did get its Silver Voice for 1943, but I can't be sure because events in my life crowded out what went on in Dobwalls. The voice of propriety, the voice of conformity, had a strength then that went far beyond the outbursts of frustrated old maids, as we all discovered when the vackies' billeting officer came and went one day. Though what followed seems antediluvian as well as inhuman to us now, it happened. I suppose all one can say is that millions of children were sent away from their parents in the evacuation and someone, somewhere had to make some rules. I was not allowed to hear what he said and he missed Uncle Jack, which was just as well. He had an order: I was not to associate with Elsie again for my 'moral welfare'. She was unmarried, fifteen, underage, and pregnant; I was ten. Breach of this could result in my being taken away from Auntie Rose and Uncle Jack, again for my 'moral welfare'. By the look of him when I saw him walking away up the Court the billeting officer had not enjoyed his mission any more than Auntie Rose had.

'Has the world gone mad?' Auntie Rose asked me rhetorically, not even seeing me before her.

Uncle Jack got home from work. He was predictably purple. 'God save us all from the clutches of the bloody Holy Ones,' he spat. 'The sooner they all join Him in heaven and leave us down yere in peace . . .' He threw his jacket across the room.

Auntie Rose went out to gather eggs while he calmed down.

I was coming out of school a day or so later when I met Mr Buckroyd. He greeted me as usual and got a half-hearted or surly response. 'What's the matter, Terry?'

'They're taking Jack and me away,' I blurted accusingly.

'Who are? Your parents?'

'No. You. The Holy Ones. And you're sending Elsie away.'

'What the devil are you talking about?'

'See? You swear too.'

The Reverend Buckroyd took a swift hand in our affairs. A phone call from him to Welling police station sent a constable to call on Mum and Dad—frightening the life out of them into the bargain. A return phone call from Dad soon settled where we should stay. But Buckroyd couldn't wave his wand over Elsie. Miss Polmanor would not tolerate a newborn illegitimate baby in her house and that was that. Elsie's father had become a prisoner of the Japanese; her mother was nowhere to be found—whether through enemy action or Allied attraction, I don't know. Elsie was bound for a home. Homes for unmarried pregnant girls appeared all over the country during the war. Somehow or another they seemed to be compulsory. Incarceration of the mother was followed by adoption of the child.

And alongside the trivia of our lives great events were taking place in the world. After the entry of the Americans in the war and our victory at El Alamein the tide had turned. North Africa was taken from Rommel; the Russians were turning defeat into triumph. British forces under the command of General Montgomery—the former Desert Rats—together with the Americans, landed on the island of Sicily. The invasion, of what Churchill mistakenly called 'the soft underbelly of Europe', had begun.

CHAPTER EIGHTEEN

Our three-year 'other childhood' came to a swift climax. With air raids more or less over, Jack was to return home to go to Woolwich Polytechnic and I was awaiting the results of the entrance exam to see if I would go to Dartford Grammar School. I heard of no plans made for me if I failed; I don't think anyone thought that would happen. The postman saw me in the Court one morning; our summer holidays had started. He handed me two envelopes and rode quickly off on his bike. The top one said 'Kent Education Committee' on it. I didn't even look at the one underneath but turned and ran indoors shouting, 'Auntie Rose, Auntie Rose, the letter's come. Look. It's come.'

She was as excited as I was. 'Well, open it, boy. Let's see.'

As I separated the two letters to open the top one I saw that the one underneath was a telegram. I stopped dead, my voice changed. 'It's a telegram.'

Her voice, indeed every angle of her body, became tense. 'Telegram? What's it say on it?'

I faltered. 'It just says "Telegram. War Office".' Any telegram was a rare enough event to send out warning signals in those days. Even I, at ten, knew the dread import of one from such a sender. The postman had shirked his duty in handing it to me. I looked at her. 'Shall I open it?'

She looked shattered, her head moving about as she looked vaguely for something. 'Where are my glasses?' There was no answer. She knocked something over. 'Oh *Duw*. Yes, open it—no—you can't—yes, open it. Read it. I can't—' She sank into a chair.

I opened it and started banally from the top. 'The War Office, Whitehall, London SW1. 8.30 a.m., 14 July 1943. We regret to inform you that your son Gwyn has been—' The word glared up at me from the telegram tape stuck onto the yellow paper. The world was reduced to that one word filling my vision. All I could manage was, 'Oh, oh.'

Auntie Rose didn't look at me. She said, almost inaudibly, 'Does it say it, boy? Does it say it? Say it doesn't.'

I just stood there staring at the word. I daren't look up at her.

She held an arm out. 'Come yere, boy. Put your arms round me. Hold me for a minute.' There was no sign of weeping. I did as she asked though she scarcely seemed to notice that I was there. 'Oh Gwyn, Gwyn, my little—I was always afraid for you. Oh Gwyn, Gwyn, Gwyn.' She started to rock back and forth still saying his name every few rocks.

After a while I said, 'Shall I go down the line and find Uncle Jack?'

'No. He'll be up from work later. Time enough for his world to end then.'

*　　　　*　　　　*

Jack and I watched Auntie Rose and Uncle Jack for two days. They didn't cling to each other or sob but their palpable misery was a bond between them that excluded us. He touched her more often

202

than usual as they moved about the room and once she laid her head against his bald one in a weary, hopeless way that seemed to fill the room with a sigh. When Auntie Rose and I were alone for some moments I took her hand, too awkward and the wrong height to embrace her properly. She put her arms round me and buried my head fiercely in her bosom. We stood there motionless while I tried not to suffocate, the only time I ever remember her needs taking precedence over mine. Jack and I crept about not knowing what to do till we went outside, over the road to the Park, and climbed up into the big beech tree to discuss it. We wrote to our parents with the result of our deliberations.

Dear Mum and Dad,

Just a line to let you know that Auntie Rose and Uncle Jack's son Gwyn has been killed in Sicily. They are very unhappy. Auntie Rose keeps crying and Uncle Jack keeps going to the bottom of the garden and just sitting there instead of going to work. We thought it would be a good idea if only one of us came home and one of us stayed here with them and became their son. Then you've both got one each. That's fair. We were going to toss for it but Jack said I've got to go back to Dartford Grammar School, Jack doesn't mind not going to the Poly and he can stay here and work on the track with Uncle Jack. He says he would like that. He could come and visit with a privilege ticket.

Love, Jack and Terry xxx

PS. I passed my entrance exam.

Another day passed. Our letter was in the post. I went and watched Uncle Jack at the bottom of the garden, beyond the outside privies. He was right at the bottom, out of sight of the houses, by the vegetables, with a cornfield beyond and the railway line rising out of its cutting and snaking towards Liskeard, Plymouth and London. I hadn't made a sound. He was sitting on an old bench set there to rest on when gardening. He had his back to me, in his own world.

'Can I come and sit with you, Uncle Jack?'

He patted the bench at once as though he had already heard me. 'Yes, come by yere, boy.' As I sat by him he ruffled what little there was of my hair. 'Time you had a haircut, is it?'

' 'S not that long.'

He was in the quietest of voices. His voice with its sharp South Wales cutting edge and its rumbling undertones was at its most gentle. 'Little blondie Anglo-Saxon. Gwyn was dark, like me: a Celt. "The soft underbelly of Europe." The mud was soft in Flanders, too. Didn't save anybody. Remember, boy: never, never, never, never, *never*, trust your leaders. Montgomery's a hero. Churchill's a hero. Gwyn is dead. And it's not just this war or the last. It's all history. "Into the Valley of Death rode the six hundred." Who sent 'em there, eh? Don't *ever* trust 'em, not any of 'em.'

Jack came round the privet hedge by the privies. 'Uncle Jack, Mr Buckroyd's with Auntie Rose. He'd like to see you too.'

'Oooh, no, not the bloody minister,' sighed Uncle Jack. 'They don't just kill you, they send someone to tell your next of kin it's all for the best.'

Mr Buckroyd came diffidently down the garden. 'Good afternoon, Mr Phillips. Boys.'

Jack and I greeted him.

Mr Buckroyd went and stood by the fence, looking out. He continued, 'I can't tell you, Mr Phillips, how sorry I—'

He was gently cut short. 'Then please don't try.'

He thought for a moment. 'I know that your wife is Church of England and that you are . . . neither, but I suggested to her a memorial service in the chapel because it is bigger there than the church, where you might have some more private gathering, and I think there would be many indeed in the village who would want to come.'

'What did she say?'

'She would like it.'

'Yes, yes, she must have it.' He gave the briefest of snorts, remembering his last performance in the chapel. It says much for Buckroyd that he was even here giving this invitation. 'Don't worry, I'll behave myself.'

'Yes, of course.'

'Only nothing about souls in heaven. Eh? Or eternal life. Or any of that. A memorial service: let's just remember him.'

'I'll vet everything myself.' He stood uncertainly, not sure how to close this meeting which had gone so easily. 'I'm sure he died a hero, Mr Phillips.'

The cliché brought an edge to Uncle Jack's voice. 'Are you, now? I seen a few o' them die. Ashes to ashes and mud to mud.' He paused and added, 'About what you did over Terry and Elsie and all that. We're very grateful. Thank you.'

'I'm doing my best about Elsie's future but it's

205

not always straightforward.'

'Yes, yes. You're a good man . . .' Uncle Jack paused. He couldn't resist it even in his agony. '. . . in spite of being a Christian.'

Buckroyd started to leave. He was stopped by Uncle Jack's raised voice.

'One other thing.' For a moment we all wondered what it could be. 'I'll apologise to Miss Polmanor when I see her.'

Buckroyd turned, surprised. 'What?'

'For calling her names. Even though she asked for it. She's just another casualty, you know. Like all of us. A million men didn't come home from the first war.' He paused. '*My* war. Huh. That left a million spare women. She was engaged, wasn't she? To a corporal in the Duke of Cornwall's Light Infantry. Killed on the Somme.'

'That's right.'

'A whole generation of leftover women. A lot of them got a bad attack of God. I suppose it's better than emptiness. She didn't want to be a dried-up old haybag. She just found out that, one day, that's what she is.'

There was a silence after this unexpected statement. Uncle Jack's arm was thrown round me. I thought, so that's who that man was in the photo, the centrepiece of the little shrine on Miss Polmanor's sideboard. Many things started to fall into place in my mind, a process that has taken years to complete, if it is complete. Mr Buckroyd was poised to go. 'You're a good man, Mr Phillips . . .' He too paused. ' . . . in spite of being an atheist.' And he was gone.

There was silence for a while.

Uncle Jack spoke. 'I like it yere, boys. Look at

206

the wind on that barley field. And the valley. And the compost heap, there, to remind us what we're coming to.'

I tried to think of anything I could. 'And the railway. That's good.'

Uncle Jack hugged me. 'Yes. That's good.' He changed tack. 'Let's have a service here. For Gwyn. Us three, eh? An Anglo-Celtic service. You remember that song you learned last year: "Barbara Allen"?'

We did.

'Sing it, both of you. Go straight to the third verse. That's suitable.'

And we sang, in two parts, me treble and Jack alto, into the summer's day, to the haunting tune of 'Barbara Allen', while Uncle Jack looked away from us into his own wounded life.

> And death is printed on his face
> And o'er his heart is stealing;
> The pain of love he bravely bore,
> So far beyond the healing.
>
> He turned his face unto the wall,
> And death was with him dealing . . .

CHAPTER NINETEEN

Two days later we faced Auntie Rose in the living room. She looked drawn and stern. 'I've got a letter yere from your mother.'

Jack spoke for us, ruefully. 'So've we.'

'You don't want to go home, is it?' she said.

I was shamefaced. 'It's not that.'

'Whose idea was it for you to stay here, then?' she pursued.

Jack was the braver of us. 'We thought it together.'

I joined in, not wanting to be thought disloyal to Auntie Rose and Uncle Jack. 'We were going to toss for it, but Jack said I've got to go back to Dartford Grammar School.'

'Did he now?' She looked at both of us with an expression I could not read. 'Come here, both of you.' She held us close. 'You're a pair, aren't you? I thought so when I first set eyes on you.' And she held us in a vice-like grip until I had to complain.

'Ow, you're hurting.'

She released us. 'But, you see, boys, you can't stay with us. As it is you both have to sleep down in the front hall there together till you go. Top 'n' tail. We must have your room at once. Don't look so pained. Guess who's going up there?'

'Soldiers?' Jack tried.

'Elsie,' said Auntie Rose. And my world exploded. 'We're going to have Elsie and her little one.'

'Elsie's going to stay here?' I said, unbelieving.

'And she'd better move in quick or they'll be shunting her off to that home, that workhouse place. That's fit for nobody, certainly not Elsie and her baby, eh?' Auntie Rose smiled at the effect she had had, her first smile for days.

'Can I go and tell her?'

'She knows, silly.'

'Well, can I go and tell her I know, too?' And I was off up the Court shouting, 'Elsie, Elsie. You're coming here, Elsie.'

*   *   *

A week later Jack and I lay in terror on our
mattress on the hall floor listening while Elsie, up
in our room with Auntie Rose and the district
nurse, gave me another lesson on the facts of life.
No excuse for me to disbelieve any longer what
went where or to puzzle how a whole baby came
out of there. We crept fearfully into the kitchen
and there was Uncle Jack with a glass in his hand.
'Hello, boy, too much of a racket to sleep, is it?
She always was a noisy girl. Now's her chance.'

'Is Elsie all right?' I asked.

'Right as rain. Here, have a sip of this. Drink to
the baby's health. Say "Good health and long life
to you."'

Jack tried a sip and had to run outside to spit it
out.

'Don't waste it,' Uncle Jack called after him.

I was concerned. 'Is it a boy or a girl?'

'A boy. Black as pitch.' Uncle Jack smiled but
without his former twinkle. That, so much a part
of him, was gone. It was like an amputation. He
contemplated some inner thought, then came back
to me. 'Well, sort of greyish really, but same
difference. Pretty little thing. I'll have to learn
some Negro spirituals to teach him for the Silver
Voice competition, eh? They're good singers,
those darkies. That Paul Robeson, he made that
film with us, didn't he: *Proud Valley*. He sang with
the South Wales miners in the Depression. Great
bass voice.' He laughed gently. 'Difficult to think
of that little scrap up there singing bass. Still.'

The whole thing was beyond me. 'Is he black—I

mean, grey—all over?'

'Just about. He'll do a lot for Rose, being yere.' His good humour faded into bitterness. 'The Lord giveth and the Lord taketh away—as the bloody minister would say.'

* * *

A few days later on Doublebois station we boarded the Cornish Riviera for Paddington. I was ten and a half when my 'other childhood' ended, Jack was nearly fifteen. We had fewer people to see us off than poor Teddy Camberwell, but there were enough: Elsie with her baby and Auntie Rose and Uncle Jack.

Oh, Auntie Rose and Uncle Jack! Ten shillings a week per vackie was the official allowance, and in return they had given themselves without stint. Was there ever such a bargain? Yes, they were about to give Elsie the same, for nothing. They were without guile and without self-interest: 'The salt of the earth' is the saying. And if ever the earth needed salting Auntie Rose and Uncle Jack were there to do it.

Amid the huffing and puffing of the engine and the stationmaster we said our farewells.

'Give my respects to your mam and dad. Write soon. Oh, we'll miss you, boys,' Auntie Rose repeated.

'Bye, Terry. See you in London one day,' said Elsie. She held up her baby's tiny hand with its pink palm. 'Say goodbye, Louis. Bye-bye. Say bye-bye.'

'Bye, Elsie. Bye, Louis.'

Doors were slammed, flags waved, a whistle

blew.

'Goodbye, Auntie Rose, Uncle Jack,' we shouted.

'Goodbye, boys. Look after your—you be—' He choked, stopped, tried to grin at us and failed miserably. Unheeded tears ran down his cheeks.

Auntie Rose cut in. 'Oh, now don't cry, Jack, for God's sake. You'll start me off.' And she started to cry.

The train moved forward.

'Remember what I said, boys,' called Uncle Jack over the noise His voice sounded urgent; he seemed suddenly afraid that we wouldn't have his distillation of what a hard life had taught him. 'Two things: it's not fair and don't ever trust 'em. Your leaders. Never. You never know what they'll do. And whatever it is, it won't be for you.'

We hung out of the window, waving furiously, and the train went past Railway Cottages above us, where neighbours were waving at the wire fence. We began to round the curve in the line so that we could only just see the platform on which Auntie Rose and Uncle Jack were standing, still waving back: last sight of our own Rock of Ages and her bloody-minded bantam.

The train took us over the Lostwithiel road, past Dobwalls, over the Moorswater Viaduct. It stopped at Liskeard, Menheniot, St Germans, Torpoint, rumbled over Saltash Bridge— presumably moving it another foot one way or the other—and we were in Plymouth, England, and on our way back to our half-forgotten home.

*　　　*　　　*

211

Uncle Jack and Auntie Rose. Auntie Rose and Uncle Jack. Aunt and uncle. Not father and mother but not distant either, just in-between relatives. In fact, of course, they weren't even that; they were our foster-mother and -father, not relatives at all. But even now, sixty-six years later, I still cannot say their names without a full heart and a lump of gratitude in my throat.

Acknowledgements

First, to my long-suffering, under-thanked, invaluable, wonderful secretary of nearly thirty years, Rae Amzallag.

To Jacky Fairclough and Mary Flanigan, granddaughters of Auntie Rose and Uncle Jack.

Wendy Barbery (née Tamblyn) of Treburgie Farm, Dobwalls.

Beth Plummer, widow of Ken, of Dobwalls.

John and Ann Roberts of Falmouth, Cornwall.

For reading early drafts: Barbara Kerr, Dominic Frisby, Eliot Watkins, Jennifer Thorne, John Hine, Sir Nigel Sweeney QC, Peter Smith LLB, Piers Croke.

Alexandra Pringle, Anna Simpson, Anya Rosenberg and all at Bloomsbury.

Lavinia Trevor and Nick Quinn, my literary agents.

My brother, Jack and his wife, Joan.

A Note on the Author

Terence Frisby is a playwright. He has worked extensively for many years as an actor, director and producer. His most famous play, *There's A Girl In My Soup*, was London's longest-running comedy and a worldwide smash hit. His script of the film, which starred Peter Sellers and Goldie Hawn, won the Writers' Guild of Great Britain Award for the Best British Comedy Screenplay. His other plays are performed internationally.

He has written many television plays and two television comedy series: *Lucky Feller* with David Jason, and *That's Love*, which won the Gold Award for Comedy at Houston IFF.

As producer, he is most proud of presenting the multi-award-winning, South African show 'Woza Albert' at the Criterion Theatre, London, subsequently off-Broadway.

His BBC Radio 4 play, *Just Remember Two Things: It's Not Fair and Don't Be Late*, from which this book sprang, won The Giles Cooper Play Of the Year Award.

A musical stage version was produced at the Queen's Theatre, Barnstaple, in 2004. Terence is currently mounting a production of it for London's West End entitled *Kisses on a Postcard*.